LOCKDOWN
Talking to Your Kids About School Violence

*Help Your Children Cope
in this Climate of Fear*

D1517800

Nancy Kislin

HIGHPOINT

This edition published by Highpoint Life.
For information, write to info@highpointpubs.com.

First Paperback Edition
ISBN: 978-1-64516-724-2

Library of Congress Cataloging-in-Publication Data

Kislin, Nancy
Lockdown: How to Talk to Your Kids About School Violence
Includes index.

Summary: "Lockdown! Talking to Your Kids About School Violence combines extensive interviews and professional therapeutic guidance for successfully nurturing and healing children in this era of school shootings. It presents strategies for emotionally preparing kids for living every day in a world with violent events in schools and elsewhere." – Provided by publisher.

ISBN: 978-1-64516-724-2 (paperback)
1. Parenting and Relationships 2. School Safety

Library of Congress Control Number: 2019930194

Design by Sarah Clarehart
Cover Art by Richard Turtletaub

Manufactured in the United States of America
10 9 8 7 6 5 4 3 2 1

LOCKDOWN
Talking to Your Kids About School Violence

Endorsements

"More than any other members of our human family, children need to feel safe. It is nearly impossible for them to focus on learning, become their best selves, and achieve their full potential when they are consumed with worry about safety. Parents, grandparents, teachers, school personnel, and religious leaders need guidance for how to help children feel safe. In *Lockdown: Talking to Your Kids about School Violence*, clinical social worker Nancy Kislin shares her own wisdom gleaned from years of experience of working with (and listening oh-so-carefully) to children, teenagers, parents, school administrators, and clergy about healthy and productive ways to discuss school violence. Ms. Kislin shares their actual words to help us gain an appreciation for the depth, breadth, and difficulty the topic of school violence presents. We wonder why we have to talk about this in the first place, but we must. School violence has become a scourge on our society. We need Ms. Kislin's timely book. Regardless of your politics, it is essential that we provide our children a safe space to explore their feelings around this topic. Our children need to be heard and spoken to with honesty and empathy. We need to offer coping strategies and solutions they can embrace. Ms. Kislin's comprehensive book offers both."
– Dale Atkins, Ph. D., psychologist, author

"In *Lockdown*, Nancy Kislin has initiated a sacred conversation that confronts a painful reality—parents, clergy, and community members must be ready to talk to young people affected by gun violence without acquiescing to a future marred by it. Importantly, Kislin emphasizes the need to empower through these interactions, encouraging young people to 'find their voice' and claim agency over the worlds they inhabit." – Rabbi Jonah Dov Pesner, Director, Religious Action Center of Reform Judaism, Senior Vice President, Union for Reform Judaism

"As a superintendent, I am forced to focus on school safety every day. Our schools' security measures include shatterproof film on the windows, swipe cards to limit access, security cameras linked to police squad cars, lockdowns,

shelter-in-place or flee-the-building drills, and guards to monitor our safety. We spend considerable funds to ensure that safety measures are kept in optimal working condition. Beyond the levels of rigor that are inherent in a high-performing district, we consider the effects our safety measures have on students. Nancy Kislin has written a book for parents, educators, and health care providers to combat these issues. Nancy addresses students' fears and anxiety in the midst of a barrage of messaging that they may be potentially involved in a school shooting. Nancy shares practical tools she uses with students to allay their panic and trepidation as they walk the halls of their schools. Nancy has provided accessible tips to support the mental health of our children while offering students the knowledge and comfort that they will be safe every day."
– **Christine Burton, Ed. D. Superintendent, Millburn Township Schools**

"Is there a voice alive today determined to acknowledge the social and psychological impact school shootings have on our children? Yes! Just read *Lockdown!* The sheer intellectual and discerning work of parenting educator and marriage and family psychotherapist Nancy Kislin provides a critical analysis and exploration on the imperative that parents, educators, and society as a whole face every day. It acknowledges the all-important need of helping our kids sift through the traumatic affects and aftermath of what has become all too common in the hallways and classrooms of American schools: fatal gunfire and mass shootings. This timely work's in-depth research and expertise offers us broader insight and reflection into the depth of the emotional impact these occurrences have on student-survivors. It also offers hope. Parents, educators, and adults everywhere will feel empowered and better equipped to engage youth in an all-important conversation concerning their genuine anxieties and fears. This work should be a welcome part of any caring parents', educators', or faith community library. It is an invaluable contribution to what it means to raise healthy kids amidst a troubled world where apathy has left us naive to the negative spiritual and psychological imprint left on our children by socio-economic, environmental, and political moral decay. Thank you, Nancy, for this countercultural witness and sacred conversation that confronts the reality of pain and provides practical advice for transformation." – **Dr. Reverend Terry Richardson, First Baptist Church of South Orange, New Jersey**

TABLE OF CONTENTS

— Contents —

Dedication

This book is dedicated to all the beautiful children who hide in corners, under desks, and in closets waiting to hear that lockdown is over.

To my daughters, I hope this book demonstrates that anything you can dream can become your reality.

Acknowledgments

Setting out on this journey to write my first book has made me confront many challenges and old wounds. I have asked myself too many times to count why someone with dyslexia would embrace this challenge. Perhaps it is the anxious little girl in me, who remembers being scared in school during fire drills, who empathizes with children hiding from a potential shooter, and who desperately wants to help them and their parents. Or, perhaps it is being a mother, terrified that I would have to bury a child. I'm also a psychotherapist who has worked with children and families for many years. I hear the fear, see the pain on the frightened faces, and know that we can all do better for our kids. My intense concern and love for children continues to fuel me on this path.

My hope is that this book helps the shy and anxious child, the exuberant child, find ways to talk about their experiences of lockdown drills with their parents and educators.

I am deeply grateful to all the children and parents who shared their experiences with me. My profound gratitude goes to my old camp friend, her lovely daughter, and many others who survived the darkest of days and were brave to share their experiences with me. All the names of students and teachers have been changed to protect their privacy.

I am forever grateful to my teachers, Randy and Robin, who continue to teach me, guide me, support me with the purest of love and care.

A special thank you to Michael Roney, my patient editor who endured my endless struggles to write this book.

I am lucky to have my life partner, friend, and editor, Rich, to hold my hand through all my adventures. His strength, kindness, and never-ending belief in me helps me achieve my dreams and goals. I also am truly blessed to have the support, love, and interminable words of encouragement from my daughters, who continue to inspire me and teach me to be the best version of myself. I love you. My gratitude extends to my mother, the strongest person I know, for living by example—demonstrating that giving to others is a gift we give ourselves, and teaching me that compassion and love are priceless.

Parents and teachers, please hear my words as a warning that many children are struggling in this climate of fear. I hope that my suggestions help you to help our children not only survive, but thrive in these scary times. My biggest hope is that not one more child has to perish due to senseless violence.

Introduction

"LOCKDOWN, LOCKDOWN, LOCKDOWN," the voice over the loudspeaker declares during school hours at least once a month. "LOCKDOWN, LOCKDOWN, LOCKDOWN." The message is repeated as the teacher runs to her classroom door, locks it, and pulls the shade down over the window. Meanwhile, the children move quickly and silently to their designated hiding place as they wait for the announcement that the drill is over. However, in those quiet moments, students do not know if it *is* a drill or the "real thing."

A few weeks after the mass shooting at Marjory Stoneman Douglas High School in Parkland, Florida, I was sitting with a fourteen-year-old student in my therapy office, talking about her stressful day. Isabelle had been coming to see me for a few months, sharing her feelings about her performance in school, accompanied by no small amount of social anxiety. Isabelle described in detail the events of the evacuation drill that occurred in school hours earlier.

"We were working on our dance routines in gym class. My group of five girls was off in the corner working on our dance when we saw lots of people running toward one end of the gym. I grabbed a boy as he was running by and asked him what was happening. He said that there was a lockdown drill. I guess our group didn't hear the announcement over the music we were playing on someone's phone. I screamed to the other girls in my group, and we all started running toward the other kids. There was a teacher by the weight room telling us to get in there. As the last kid entered, she slammed the door, barricading us in that smelly place with chairs and weight equipment, and we waited to see what would happen. Luckily, some kids had their phones and were texting other students to see what was going on.

"After a few minutes, someone learned via text from another student that what was happening was not a lockdown drill, but an evacuation drill. But it wasn't a drill.

"Before I had time to panic, kids stripped away the barricade and the teacher opened the door. It was eerie how quiet the gym was. Another teacher happened to be running through the gym heading toward the exit when he saw all of us. He screamed, 'WHAT ARE YOU DOING THERE? GET OUT!' He and my teacher brought us out of the weight room and led us to the nearest door going to the outside. Just as we got outside, another teacher loudly said, 'This is not a drill! Go to the outer field NOW!'

"Most of us just starting running and running until we were far away from the school. When I finally caught my breath, I realized that there were sirens going off and I could see police near the school."

Wow. This was quite a story from a teen that doesn't usually talk very much. I asked what happened next. She replied, "Oh, apparently there were some contractors working in the building. One man left his backpack unattended; there were wires hanging out of the bag. Someone thought it may have been a bomb."

⋙◆⋘

One Sunday I was taking a walk around a lake near my home and couldn't help but overhear the young man in front of me ask his mom, "If someone got shot out here, how long do you think it would take for an ambulance to come to help him?"

The mother turned to the kid, "What is with you and guns? All you do is talk about guns and getting shot."

As the mom and son walked further along the shoreline, I couldn't actually hear anything else they were saying. Although the one thing I *had heard* certainly was troubling, on some level it actually gave me hope that at least some kids and parents were talking with one another about one of the most vexing issues in our society.

As a therapist who has worked with teens for the last three decades, I had a blueprint for how to help parents navigate the teen years. Hearing these stories made me realize I needed to amend it.

Today's Sad Reality

The sad reality is that school children everywhere live with the long-lasting trauma of bearing witness to a school shooting. Even just enduring lockdown drills can be traumatic. The statistics are disturbing: Approximately 187,000 school children have been exposed to gun violence since the Columbine school shooting in 1999, according to *The Washington Post*.[1] Thirteen students died at Columbine High School, twenty-six in the Sandy Hook school shooting, and seventeen at Marjory Stoneman Douglas High School in Parkland.

These days, students learn about the news in real time. A school shooting happens in Florida and a teen in California is hyper-focused on how many kids are dead as he stares hopelessly at the screen of his smartphone during class. He wonders, "Could this happen here?" or even, "When will this happen at my school?" or, "My mom has family in Florida—I wonder if anyone we know is there. Oh no, now my mom is going to worry even more about me going out . . ." His mind weaves an intricate web of fear.

This is now a world in which it is commonplace for high school students to discuss whether jumping out of a second-floor classroom window is better than getting shot by an intruder. Children are coming of age in a time when the basic assumption, "I will be safe in school" no longer holds true.

What Can We Do About This?

After asking many students about their experiences during lockdown

---

[1] John Woodrow Cox and Steven Rich, "Scared by School Shootings," *The Washington Post*, March 25, 2018, https://www.washingtonpost.com/graphics/2018/local/us-school-shootings-history/?utm_term=.e2f12125468c.

drills, evacuation drills, and active shooter drills, I became intensely curious about what consequences this is having on children. I wondered if parents were aware of what each lockdown drill entails. I also wanted to know how the epidemic of school shootings was impacting school staff, particularly teachers.

My concerns included the following:

+ Were parents aware of the experiences their kids were having on a regular basis due to ongoing drills, and what (hopefully) turns out to be false alarms?

+ How was this environment affecting kids who engaged in the monthly exercise of playing "hide and seek" from a madman with a gun?

+ Was society becoming numb to the fact that guns are killing children every day?

+ School shootings are at an all-time high, and there are constant reports of kids coming to school with loaded guns. Have we grown weary to the issue of gun violence?

+ Was the fear of school shootings creating a generation of children who are at greater risk of suffering from anxiety, depression, and other mental health issues?

+ Did parents and children really believe that there was nowhere safe anymore? Was this causing anxiety? Depression? Self-harming behavior? Was it creating a sense of hopelessness in children?

+ Was the fear of school violence resulting in parents becoming more overprotective, thus robbing their children of the opportunity to develop a strong identity separate from them?

I was also particularly interested in how American children, parents, and school staff were handling lockdown drills.

+ What was it like for kids to have the ongoing experiences of lockdown drills, intruder drills, fire drills, and evacuation drills at least once a month at their schools?

+ Were schools required to have drills a certain number of times per year?

+ Were drills effective in keeping children safe during a real shooting?

+ Were teachers and administrators prepared to handle these situations?

+ How were parents handling the topic of guns killing innocent children and the "need" for drills to be happening in schools?

As a psychotherapist and mother, I started interviewing superintendents, school principals, and teachers to help me understand what it is like from their perspective. I spoke with parents whose children survived school shootings. How did they feel about the drills? Were they afraid it would happen in their school? What precautions did they take to prevent a school shooting? How did they communicate with parents about the school lockdown drills?

I extended my questioning to include pediatricians, child and adolescent psychiatrists, colleagues, camp directors, and college educators. My investigation naturally grew in scope to cover something much broader: the trauma that school shootings are causing all of our kids, and how, despite it all, we can prepare and nurture them to grow up happy and resilient.

What I have found is that many parents are terrified to send their kids to school and are not doing a great job of hiding their fears from their children. Many kids worry about their own safety and if their parents can handle all this stress.

I also have discovered a huge breakdown in communication between parents and their children about the dread and anxiety experienced by kids having to run and hide in a broom closet or under a desk, fearing that they or their friends could be killed.

There is a disconnect between what children are experiencing in school and what parents understand to be happening. Most parents with whom I spoke had no idea that their children were hiding behind metal cabinets or crammed into a storage closet in total darkness as they waited to find out if it was just a drill or the real thing.

I didn't know that was how lockdown drills were happening, so I wondered if other parents knew that each month or so their kids were actively preparing to avoid being shot to death. My research revealed that many public schools have one lockdown drill per month, while private schools and preschools have no such requirement. The following are types of lockdown drills and their purpose:

- **Lockdown:** Isolate students and staff from threats of violence such as suspicious trespassers or armed intruders that may occur in a school or in the vicinity of a school.

- **Shelter-in-Place:** Limit the exposure of students and staff to hazardous materials such as chemical, biological, or radiological contaminants released into the environment by isolating the inside environment from the outside.

- **Evacuation:** Move students and staff away from threats such as fires, oil train spills, or tsunamis.[2]

Most public schools coordinate their drills with local police who are often present during drills. At the time of my investigation, school safety and drills were regulated by individual states.

Many of the children I interviewed seemed very grateful to have the opportunity to talk about their experiences during drills. They seemed relieved to share their stories and to hear me acknowledge how hard it must be to stay quiet when you wonder if the drill is indeed just a drill.

Parents' reactions to my questions ranged from intense concern that the drills are harmful to their kids but they know they are required, to parents not realizing their kids even had drills. Many parents said they thought their kids were "fine," and that lockdown drills were normal and didn't bother the children. But I wasn't sure if that was really the kids' feelings.

---

[2] http://www.k12.wa.us/safetycenter/Drills/default.aspx

There seems to be a pattern of parents sharing their concerns with their children; "I couldn't handle it if something happened to you in a school shooting." This only adds to a child's struggle with the fear of whether or not each drill is the real thing.

This book is the result of my personal exploration into this serious situation.

The Voices of Parkland

Ella sat quietly on the couch tightly holding onto the pillow that rested on her lap. She looked anxiously around the room, glancing periodically back and forth at her girlfriends. The girls referred to themselves as a very tight group of friends. They had all been in school that deadly day in February, 2018.

The girls and I were gathered in a beautiful home in the idyllic community of Parkland. Ella shared with me something she worries about. "No one goes to the bathroom during class anymore. We are all too scared. Really, no one in any of my classes leaves the classroom anymore. If someone has to go to the office or to the nurse, we go with a friend."

Maggie, who had been quiet during most of the interview, added, "It's too scary. What if a drill happens when I am in the hallway or in the bathroom?"

The girls explained that school policy states if you are in the hallway and a drill is announced, you have to run into the nearest classroom. Lani jumps in with, "I am not going into a classroom where I don't know anyone. That is so creepy. What happens if there is a shooter and we have to hide? I don't want to be alone with people I don't know."

Savannah said that if you are caught in the bathroom during a lockdown drill, you have to hide in the stall and put your feet up on the toilet. "I would be terrified to be in there by myself. I don't want to die alone."

All of the girls nodded.

On the surface, this could have been any living room in America with me talking to the girls about boys, drugs, or school pressure, but that was not what was happening here. I was sitting with survivors of the worst mass school shooting to happen on American soil.

Maggie was concerned that I understand how the bathroom situation was a big deal. She stated that there was a guy who came out of the bathroom on the day of the shooting. He walked out only to see the shooter loading bullets into his gun. The shooter looked right at him and then turned back to shooting up the class. The guy was able to run back into the bathroom. "Can you believe it? He didn't die," she added.

I asked the girls, "How are you all doing?"

There were some grunts and shrugs. Lara's haunting eyes looked at me for a few seconds and then glanced down to the carpet and back at me. Her hands clasped a pillow tightly as she quietly stated, "I had a panic attack in class today."

I asked, "Why the panic attack?"

"We had a fire drill today. It happened late in the day, just like it did *that* day. Right after the shooting, they changed the sound of all the bells in the school—the class bell, the fire alarm bell—and added all types of precautions to try and stop what happened the last time. We have been instructed that we are only to leave our classrooms when we hear the fire alarm sirens after one of the administrators gets on the loudspeaker and states this is a real drill. 'Exit your classrooms.' The new alarm went off. Everyone froze—we all looked at each other waiting for the administrator to get on the PA system and say this is a fire drill. Silence. We waited. We did not hear the announcement that it was a drill. I freaked out.

"Finally, someone came on the PA and said 'this is the real thing—an unplanned drill.' We had to evacuate. I was terrified.

"It turned out that a kid pulled the alarm. But it took a long time before most of us students knew what was going on. I was so scared as we ran through the halls and outside."

On February 14, 2018, a former student pulled the fire alarm in the school. As the students were returning to class, he started shooting. On that day, months later, I looked at the sweet young woman sitting before me and saw the fear and trauma that embodied her. She courageously let me see a glimpse of the nightmare that was still plaguing her months after the school shooting that robbed seventeen members in her community of their lives.

I looked around the room at all of these brave girls, shaking my head in disbelief that one horrific day permanently altered their childhood. A sense of innocence and safety was lost that day.

The Empty Chair

As the conversation with the teens from Marjory Stoneman Douglas High School was drawing to a close, a question I had not planned to ask just popped out of my mouth. I couldn't help myself.

As I felt the heaviness, the pain, and the anxious movements of the girls who more than anything just wanted to be okay, I uttered one word.

"Guilt?"

The energy in the room changed. Dead silence for a few seconds as they all nodded. One brave soul whispered, "Every day, all the time."

Once she said this, it was as if she gave them permission to speak and feel and they all chimed in. "How could we not?" one whispered. Another girl added, "Why did they die and I didn't?"

This may sound cliché to you, but this is their reality. It is the stuff their nightmares are about.

"One of the boys who was killed was in my science class," said Jane. "I didn't know him very well. When we finally came back to school it was so weird to see his empty chair. My teacher never said anything about him dying or the school shooting. He said nothing. It was so weird." Jane continued to say that it was really difficult to go into her science class and just see that empty chair.

Jane added that her other teachers talked about the shooting. "We didn't get much work done in her class but we talked about how we were doing, how we were feeling. It was my favorite class. Nothing was normal after that day, so why should some teachers pretend as if it was?"

Teachers didn't know what to do. I don't fault the science teacher. No one is prepared to handle one of their students being killed at school. Is there a manual of what to do after one of your students gets shot and dies in your classroom? (You will learn more about this in Chapter 5, "Talking to Your Kids About Violence.")

Panic Attacks

"I thought I was going to throw up!" exclaimed Ella. "I was so scared I just kept thinking I was going to lose it all over this closet."

The girls present added several more observations:

"There were about thirty of us hiding in a small closet. One girl was sobbing; her phone was only at 5 percent. I didn't know her. She was desperate to talk to her parents. I just gave her my battery charger and said 'use it.' I already spoke to my parents. I didn't want her not to talk to them, you know."

"I never wore the shoes or the clothes I had on that day."

"We had to stay in the room until they found him."

"Teachers kept asking us kids, 'What are you guys hearing?' They did not have their phones."

"My sister sent me a picture of the shooter while I was still hiding in the closet. I knew who was shooting up my school when I was still hiding."

"I freak out every time I hear a helicopter. We could hear all the helicopters flying overhead that day."

"I freaked out in my seat. Everyone looked calm but me."

"I didn't sleep a lot for a long time. "

"Someone played a certain song on the bus during my summer trip and I lost it."

"My parents are having a hard time. They keep saying they never thought something would happen here."

"It just starts. I start panicking. I try to tell myself I am fine. But then I am not okay. Getting anxious. I need this to stop."

"My panic attacks are triggered by sounds, thoughts, helicopters. I heard a helicopter yesterday overhead and freaked. Then I realized, '*Oh, it's just a helicopter.*'"

"I panic when I am alone or if a place is too crowded. I won't walk alone to my car. Actually, I won't go alone anywhere by myself. I will find someone to go with."

"We were so lucky we were together in the media closet. We were so worried that our friends were okay. We kept texting each other. We knew…" she points to two of her friends, "We knew they were in a different closet together in another room. We could hear the gunshots. It was terrifying."

"If we didn't have our phones we would have gone insane. Even though people were saying all kinds of incorrect information, at least we were in contact with others."

I asked the girls how their parents were doing. "My mom is so careful with me. She needs to know how I am, where I am all the time. It's okay. I get it."

Taking Action

I must admit that after talking to so many kids and parents, I'm keeping an eye on the movement that was started by the teens of Parkland, Florida. I continue to hope that we are a country that is moving toward change.

The status quo isn't good enough for our kids. It cannot be okay to have children grow up consumed with worry about guns killing their families and friends.

I will not forget the interview I had with Tania, a fourteen-year-old from New Jersey. When I asked if she worried about someone coming to her school with a gun, she looked directly at me and said, "I am always worried. I worry when I walk to school that I could get shot by a random person, and I worry in school that a crazy man will come and shoot up my school. I remember being a little girl and not being afraid to play outside. I wished for those days again, before I knew how much danger existed in the world."

We must do better for Tania and all children.

It was after listening to brave children, teens, and teachers describe what they and millions of other school children endure every month that I decided to write this book. I hope that it will help your family find balance in how to talk with your kids, what to say, how to set healthy boundaries, and how to help your child talk about, understand, and not be terrified by their experiences.

I hope that the young activists stirring up the long-overdue conversation about gun safety in America will help to make students safer in their schools and in their homes. I hope that this book will inspire you to talk to your kids about their personal experiences during lockdown drills.

Most of all, I hope that this book arms you with the knowledge that you can help your child grow up in a world feeling safe and loved.

CHAPTER 1

What Is Really Going on with Your Kids?

We're in a crisis situation: School children are being traumatized by monthly lockdown drills, evacuation drills, and drills on what to do if an active shooter enters the school before a lockdown takes place.

In many states throughout the country, public schools are mandated to have a lockdown, an evacuation, or shelter-in-place drill once a month. This is in addition to fire drills. My research has led to me to conclude that some schools alert the children that it is a drill, while others pretend that it is the real thing until the drill is over. Regardless of the type of drill, they all are disruptive, confusing, frightening, often overwhelming, and for some, even traumatizing.

I want you to understand the specifics of the drills in order to talk to your kids about this practice.

In my interviews for this book, I found parents who either have no idea what was happening to their kids during these drills, or who thought they had an idea until their children explained the specifics of the event.

Parents, you need to be aware of what is happening to your kids during lockdown drills. You need to help your children recognize that the fantasies they create in their minds during the lockdown drills have an emotional impact.

Unfortunately, during hundreds of interviews, my fear was confirmed: Many parents did not realize the frequency of the drills and underestimated the degree of trauma they were causing their children.

Sarah, a friendly mom with children aged fourteen, eleven, and eight, told me that she tries to remember to check in with them about their school's lockdown drills, but sometimes she forgets. She said that recently her eleven-year-old told her he was upset when the last drill occurred.

I asked Sarah if I could speak directly with her children. After talking with them, I learned that their school had recently changed the drill policy. In the past, they would play a certain song over the loudspeaker to alert the children and teachers that there was a lockdown in place. Since the shooting in Parkland, things have become more serious according to the eleven-year-old. "Now, a voice on the loudspeaker says 'CODE RED, CODE RED,' and everyone runs to their hiding places. Some kids hide in the cabinets, but our classroom doesn't have any so we all huddle together. One girl got so upset, she was crying and crying. We had to wait for over an hour for someone to knock on our classroom door and enter to tell us it was all safe."

An hour! Think about it: A group of children huddled in a classroom in a suburban New Jersey elementary school, not knowing if they were safe or about to become victims of a violent crime! Unfortunately, this scene is being played out in classrooms throughout our country.

During a discussion with fourteen-year-old Brittany, I learned that some teachers are often unable to cover up their own fears about a potential school shooting. Brittany described how her eighth-grade English teacher "freaked out" during the last drill they had in class. She recalled that as soon as the announcement was heard, the teacher screamed "Hide, hide kids!" as she dove under her desk. She left the assistant teacher to run to the door to lock it, go to the windows and lower the shades, and encourage other students to hide. Brittany was anxiously giggling as she described what seemed like a chaotic scene. Brittany's mom absorbed her story in wide-eyed disbelief.

To be clear, I am not placing blame on the teachers. To me, Brittany's account provides evidence that all school staff, students, and parents need greater education on this subject and in dealing every day with the emotional unease brought on by school violence, particularly senseless shootings.

Brian, a passionate high school teacher, gave me his thoughts on lockdown drills. He said that after the shooting in Parkland, his school started giving the teachers a heads-up in the morning that there was going to be a drill. By the time it happened, everyone, including the students, knew it was a drill.

I asked him what the experience of going through the drill felt like. He answered, "It became very routine for me. I knew it was coming. I knew what I had to do, and I was just waiting for it to be over.

"In my school, our doors open out into the hallways. I make sure to pull the door in and lock it. I turn off the lights. We used to have to make sure the windows were locked, but now that is up for discussion. There is a lot of discussion among school administrators and police that it may be safer for the students to exit through the windows than to wait for a shooter to come and assassinate us."

I asked, "What do the kids do?"

"The kids are supposed to run to the farthest place from the door and be away from the windows. That means that all the kids and I run to the back corner. Some try to fit under the desks, but most are just in a big huddle."

"Are they on their phones?"

"Yes, they all pull out their phones."

My mouth dropped. In all the months I had been interviewing teachers, parents, and students, I never envisioned them hiding under desks or in big huddles, all the while staring at their phones during a lockdown drill. I had imagined the kids seeking out comfort from their friends and classmates, and hoped that this common experience would serve to bring some of them together in comfort.

This image of those kids should serve as an alarm bell for you, too!

It is a tragedy that this generation of children has to experience this trauma. It's sad that this only highlights a cultural norm that is resulting in more children feeling alienated, not good enough, depressed, and anxious, without the tools to manage or convey those feelings.

I asked another teacher if he allowed the students to have their phones out during the drills. "Yes," he answered.

"What if it was a real crisis—don't you worry that the kids could be distracted by what they are doing on the phone and that they won't pay attention to impending danger?"

He said he had never thought of that. "I felt like it was okay for the kids to be distracted until the drill was over."

The Problem Today

The difficult truth is that lockdown drills are only one factor in an environment ripe for traumatized, emotionally unhealthy children.

The key to raising healthy, emotionally grounded children in what seems to be an increasingly violent world begins at home, but the majority of kids today are not being raised to become resilient, independent, passionate, and self-confident people. That's because the role of the parent has changed drastically in the last two decades to the point that the concept of what constitutes family life has completely been altered.

Technology Is Causing Major Issues

Let's start with the obvious. Parents are addicted to technology and so are their kids. But does playing video games actually contribute to an increase in violent behaviors? Social media and video games often are much more appealing than just interacting with one another the "old-fashioned way," as one human to another. Jean Twenge, in her book *iGen*, notes that the smartphone itself is less the issue than the larger culture of adolescence and how teens interact with one another via social media. Dr. Twenge states that we should ask what else about our culture has shifted in the last decade, as we all have become more connected and more vulnerable to changes brought on by technology.[1] She asks us to examine the role of education in the ever-changing frontier of children's

---

[1] Beverly Amico, "Education's Role in Curbing Teen Anxiety," Essentials in Education Blog, https://blog.waldorfeducation.org/2018/02/educations-role-in-curbing-teen-anxiety.

lives. Although she is a proponent of screen time limits, she realizes that there is much more to the story than that.

Additionally, it feels as if every week there is further research supporting the connection between violent video gaming or watching violence in some form, and how it can lead to unhealthy behavior. Both the American Psychological Association (APA) and the American Academy of Pediatrics (AAP) have taken a firm stance against children and teens playing violent video games.

In 2017, APA's Task Force Assessment of Violent Video Games published a study as part of its effort to update its policy about the impact violent video game use has on potentially aggressive and violent behaviors. It found that the use of violent video games results in an overall increase in aggression as well as increases in the individual variables of aggressive behaviors, aggressive cognitions, aggressive affect, desensitization, and physiological arousal, along with decreases in empathy. It did not find sufficient studies to evaluate whether there actually is a link between violent video game use and criminal behavior, and recommends additional research in a variety of areas, including more studies of younger children, those of different ethnicities and genders, dose-response effects, and game characteristics. However, the study did conclude that violent video game use is a risk factor for subsequent aggression.[2]

The American Academy of Pediatrics also concluded that existing data show a significant link between virtual violence and aggression.[3]

This isn't good news, but the full implications of virtual violence are best understood by looking at population levels. Although the majority of Americans believe there is a connection between screen violence and real-world aggression, many feel that they and their children are immune to these effects. The so-called third-person effect causes people to believe

---

[2] Sandra L. Calvert, Kenneth A. Dodge, Gordon C. Nagayama Hall, et al, "The American Psychological Association Task Force Assessment of Violent Video Games: Science in the Service of Public Interest," American Psychologist, 2017. https://public.psych.iastate.edu/caa/VGVpolicyDocs/17CalvertAPA-MVtaskforce.pdf

[3] http://pediatrics.aappublications.org/content/138/2/e20161298.

that a small, susceptible fraction of people, but not themselves, are influenced in a way the majority of the population is not. Assuming that this belief is true, even if it only 2 percent of the population is influenced to behave more aggressively after being exposed to violent media, we can expect that 400,000 of the 20 million viewers of the latest violent blockbuster will exhibit increased aggression after viewing the movie, at least for a short period of time. As a parent, I hope this causes you to think about what you are letting your children view and play. (I discuss more about the effects of technology in Chapter 4, "Virtual Violence: Is It Really Bad?")

Lack of Responsibility

Due to all of this technology, it has become ever more difficult for parents to build relationships with their children that foster opportunities to learn and grow—helping them develop a sense of confidence, independence, and resilience. Performing chores and holding a job are examples of how a child learns to thrive and push through challenging and uncomfortable situations.

I have worked with hundreds of parents who push back when I suggest that they give their kids chores. I get comments such as, "My child has so much homework" or, "We would rather he focus on his schoolwork." I have heard this excuse for kids as young as eight years old, and as old as seventeen. Parents don't realize this doesn't help a child build inner strength. Neither does giving your kids twenty dollars every time they want to go out, or filling out their admissions application yourself when they apply for college.

For several years now, parenting has shifted toward putting children up on pedestals. This includes the habit that many parents have of giving their children trophies for simply showing up in a competitive activity, just because they are so worried about hurt feelings in the event that someone else's child happens to receive a performance-based award and for some reason theirs doesn't. Parents seem to have lost their way, thinking that devoting their existence to how many friends their children have, to how many sporting or musical awards they receive, to how many Instagram followers they have, or to what college they get into, is a reflection on them. The scale has tipped so dramatically in the last ten-plus years that we finally are seeing the error of our ways—that our actions are leading to a generation of children who are complacent, addicted to devices, self-absorbed, unhappy, and lack coping skills.

In fact, there are many reports stating what those of us in the field of mental health and education of our youth already know: A record number of children and teens are anxious and depressed. They are being put in scary, confusing, unsettling situations at school, and most parents have no idea what is going on. Also, while parents are "over-involved" in some ways, they are not talking to their kids about lockdowns. While schools react to the crisis of shootings by trying to keep children safe, they often leave parents out of the conversation.

Hyper-Vigilance Is Causing Stress

Gun violence is causing children to be hyper-vigilant even when they don't need to be—training their brains to constantly be on alert. It is literally altering how they experience the world, and is negatively impacting their trust in themselves and adults, including their parents and teachers.

This constant state of high alert creates stress in the body and produces too much cortisol, which affects numerous body functions including blood-sugar levels, metabolism, inflammation, and memory. It makes it more difficult to experience joy. Equally as important is the fact that it robs children of learning how to live in the moment, experience joy, and relax.

It used to be that children did not always have to worry about whether they were safe or not. Many adults savor memories of spending days playing outside, going to the park, walking in the woods, or hanging out in a friend's backyard until the sun set. Our parents had a general idea of where we were and who we were with. Even the most anxious of our parents let their kids play outside.

In the last ten to fifteen years, this behavior of letting children have a sense of freedom to explore the world on their own, yet within the bounds of their community, has all but disappeared. I don't believe it is because the world has become more dangerous in most towns, but because parents have become more anxious and fearful. Parents divulge their own concerns to their children, often squashing the child's sense of curiosity and adventure.

Are You Questioning Your Parenting?

The current climate of mass shootings and other gun violence is one of the many things that has caused many moms and dads to question the effectiveness of their parenting style. It is normal for some children to feel reluctant and even fearful about going to school, especially in elementary grades. Often, if there is turmoil in the home, illness, financial issues, or abuse, children may become attached to one or both parents and fearful to leave their home. Once children are in middle school or high school, resistance to attending school, known as school avoidance, is an indication that something is amiss in the child's life. This is a good time to involve the school and possibly mental health experts.

One parent shared with me her deep concern that her daughter had a constant fear—something terrible could happen to someone she loves.

Many parents feel overwhelmed with the challenges they face today.

Mom stated, "My daughter gets so anxious during class that she texts me to let me know that she has a headache, a stomach ache, or is worried about taking a test, and feels better once I answer her back. If I don't answer right away, she will send me frantic texts:'What happened to you, where are you, are you okay?'" If a child is consumed by her fear, focused on receiving a text back from her mom, I doubt she is learning much at school.

Many parents feel overwhelmed with the challenges they face today. For them, it is a constant battle—from what video games their children want to play on their devices, or how much time they spend on them, to their kids' resistance to play outdoors. Many worry about their child isolating themselves in their bedrooms to be left alone with electronic "friends."

Parents are worn out from these battles, and kids' addiction to technology is the single most common problem they face. Many have given up before the battle has begun, feeling helpless that they cannot control their child's behavior. This is dangerous. It also bleeds into many other areas of parenting, including this discussion. If parents feel that they cannot stop their children from playing on their devices too much, or from engaging in illegal behavior such as vaping (use of an electronic cigarette to inhale tobacco or marijuana) or drinking, then they have essentially surrendered their power. This can cause children to feel isolated, emotionally abandoned, and alone with their thoughts. Without having an adult to help discuss and decipher their ideas, many kids will create scary, dark stories in their minds that worry them.

What Can You Do?

What can you do about all of this? How can you talk to your kids and help them negotiate these scary times? How can you aid them to feel safe and help them maintain a joyful, positive view of life that is so critical to their wellbeing?

Start with this thought: Kids would be calmer if their parents were calmer. Sorry, but it is usually the truth. This is a good time for you to examine how you are doing in that department. So how are you doing? I get it. It is a really scary world out there, and I know you feel it is your job to keep your child safe at all times. But the truth is, you can't micromanage every minute of their lives with 100 percent certainty that they will never be in danger.

It also is your job to raise a confident, happy child who is kind, giving, and helps to make the world a better place.

Your Reality Check

Parents who treat their children as fragile objects that must be dusted off, put on a pedestal, and have every whim attended to are in for a rough time.

You need a reality check. When was the last time you made time for you and your partner—for a date, a walk, or other quality together time? This is a good place to start! It not only is good for you but also teaches your child that taking care of yourself is paramount for living a happy and healthy life.

Kids would be calmer if their parents were calmer.

Do you constantly keep the news station on in your car and house? Turn it off. It is filling your head with noise of doom and gloom. You are training yourself to be prepared for the next "breaking news" cycle, most likely featuring a violent act or a horrific natural disaster. Are you one of those parents who can't wait to relay news of horror to your family as soon as one of them walks through the door at night?

Stop and ask yourself: What are you doing, and why?

You are injecting fear, and maybe even a sense of hopelessness, into your child's mind. Being constantly exposed to your anxious feelings, as well as absorbing the world's problems, is often too much for most kids. It serves no purpose.

While speaking with Leigh, a fourteen-year-old girl, it was obvious that she was struggling with a high level of anxiety; a constant theme was around the fear of being safe. Leigh reluctantly shared that she was afraid to walk to school or even to a nearby friend's home by herself. When I asked her "Why?" she simply stated that someone could abduct her. Leigh lives in a small town with an almost 0 percent crime rate.

Although Leigh and her mom are not my clients, I would not hesitate to guess that Mom, Dad, or both of them have a lot of anxiety that they have directly and indirectly imparted to their daughter. When children grow up in an environment that teaches caution and apprehension to new activities, and they don't have some professionally based guidance to help them process their emotions, it often leads to a path of anxiety.

The Difficult Discussion: Finding a Balance

Parents with whom I've spoken in schools, workshops, community events, and even through my private practice, struggle with how to find the right balance between protecting their children from today's dangers and going to the other extreme of creating fragile, fearful, and hopeless kids. That is only making the problem worse.

Fear and anxiety develop when we don't have the opportunity to talk about how something makes us feel, or something we don't understand occurs. There is a good chance your child is picking up on your fears, as well as having their own worries.

So what can you do? How do you interact with your kids on this most sensitive and critical of topics? How do you say the right things to protect their safety while nurturing their confidence, happiness, and overall emotional well-being?

"Hey Mom, did you know there was a school shooting?"

Recently, I spoke at a parenting forum on the topic, "Talking to Your Children in This Climate of Fear." I asked the audience for questions, and a woman in the front row raised her hand and stated that she came to the workshop because she was conflicted. She had chosen not to speak to her children about the school shooting in Parkland on February 14, 2018. Then, a few weeks later, while picking up her eleven-year-old child and his younger siblings from school, her son walked up and asked, "Hey Mom, did you know there was a school shooting?"

She briefly acknowledged her child's comments, and quickly ushered him into the car. She told us that she was concerned that other parents standing nearby would be angry that her son had essentially just announced the tragedy to all of them.

I suggested that she think about how her child may have felt when he first learned of the shooting. How did he handle learning that innocent kids were killed while they were in school? Who could he talk to about the experience? Did he wonder why his mom and dad didn't speak with him about the shooting? Were they trying to protect him, thinking he was too young or too immature to handle the news? Or were his parents worried that it would happen at his school? Did they think he may get killed?

See how easy it is for an idea to snowball into a scary story? It is a good strategy to speak about a situation that your child is more than likely to hear.

When a parent speaks directly about what I call "taboo" subjects, it gives the child the opportunity to build trust in their parents, to learn to ask questions in a safe and non-judgmental place. It also gives the parent the opportunity to monitor how the child handles certain information.

Dealing with Hard Topics

The prospect of dealing with the spate of violence—especially in schools—is paralyzing to some, while others go overboard in the opposite direction. I spoke with my niece, who is an alumnus of Marjory Stoneman Douglas High School, right after the news broke about the shooting. She is the mother of three young children. She described in detail how much security was in place when she went to pick up her daughters from pre-school that afternoon and since then. A few days after the shooting, she told me that her older daughter, age five, was inquiring about why it took so long to get into her school now, and why there were so many police people.

I asked my niece, "What did you say?"

What *do* parents say at times like this?

I imagine these types of scenarios are common. In fact, many smart, kind, loving, devoted parents have a hard time talking to their kids about school violence, and many avoid it all together. However, talking to your kids about these things is essential. Avoiding tough situations is not helpful to kids. It leaves them feeling they are alone in their thoughts, with a blank canvas on which they create scary stories and images—especially since so many children these days are constantly exposed to violent videos, movies, and yes, everyday news reports. Unfortunately, our kids have plenty of material available to them, intensifying their fears.

Parents' reluctance is understandable. Many report to me that their kids know what is happening in the world. "We keep the news on in the car, and it's always on the TV at home," shared one mom. After hearing this, I started to include this question in interviews with kids and their parents: "Do you listen to or watch the news?" I learned that many parents assume kids aren't listening because they are engaged in their devices, but this is not true. Kids hear and see much more than parents may think.

I provide detailed guidance for these types of discussions in Chapter 5, "Talking to Your Kids About Violence."

The Benefits of Boredom

It is important for children to be bored. That's because a child's healthy development depends on learning the skill of entertaining oneself and being comfortable without the need for external distractions. If a young person is always connected to friends on a device, for example, he or she is being deprived of this key attribute.

I started working with a sixteen-year-old boy and his parents after he had gotten suspended from school for vaping in the bathroom and possessing marijuana. The parents, obviously upset, were looking for guidance on how to help their son. The father grounded the boy for two months, which included no video gaming. The son's outrage was intense. He was terrified about what he would do without having access to his games, or to the community of virtual friends with whom he plays. To him, it seemed like the worst thing his parents could do.

I acknowledged the boy's fear. With some coaching, he was able to articulate that he was afraid that he would not be able to tolerate being disconnected from his gaming community. I suggested he could use this time to catch up on school work, get more physically active, and read. When I said that, he shot me a death look. "Read! Why would I do that?"

I answered, "Oh, do you not like to read?"

"No . . . well, I don't know. Nobody reads."

Still trying to engage him in conversation to learn more about where all this fear was coming from, I asked, "What are some of your favorite books?"

Silence. (And by the way, this is a kid who gets good grades at an affluent and competitive school district.)

Me: "Have you read . . .?"

Silence again.

A few grumbles and then, "Well, I don't really read the books for school. You know, there are SparkNotes, and kids share homework these days."

I often suggest that kids try listening to books on tape if they don't like to read, but that doesn't seem to be popular, either. A majority of kids would rather engage in social media, play video games, and watch other people playing video games on YouTube than read.

What Really Is Going On

Overall, American children are not interested in reading, or even playing if it isn't on a screen, and consequently, they struggle with critical and creative thinking.

In a world where information is literally at our kids' fingertips, it is imperative to acknowledge that many children are not thriving. The rates of suicide, depression, and anxiety are increasing, with more and more twentysomethings moving back home, unable to succeed on their own.

It all comes down to this: If you are still fortunate to be raising children, don't be afraid to be the parent. It is a huge challenge in this scary world, but I am here to guide you through this difficult terrain.

CHAPTER 2

Trauma from the Mouths of Babes

After the school shooting in Parkland, Florida, my impression was that kids throughout our country believed that their school was next. Living in fear of impending death obviously would be traumatic for children. A few weeks after the shooting, I began talking to students to see how they were managing in this climate of fear.

My experience as a therapist is that kids will talk to me when I show I am interested in what they have to say about their pets, video games, bikes, and even the annoying things their siblings do. Under the right circumstances, they also are willing to talk about the trauma of school shootings and lockdown drills.

It did not come as any surprise to me that the majority of the kids I interviewed for this book seemed to answer my questions honestly. The trick of getting a kid to talk to you is all in how you engage them in conversation. For me, this has always been easy. I simply look them in the eyes, make sure I am on their level, and let them know I really do care about what they have to say.

I've observed that the majority of school children at every age are being affected by feelings of anxiety and fear, so when it comes to school shootings, keeping them safe and healthy means that we *must* engage with them in an ongoing conversation.

First-Grader Molly and the Lockdown Drill

During a conversation among parents and kids one evening on my neighborhood street, Molly, a spunky first-grader, told me that sometimes her class is instructed that a lockdown is a drill, but other times she doesn't know if it is a drill or the real thing.

Molly articulately described how a lockdown drill proceeds. She told me that her teacher runs to the door, locks it, then hastens to the windows and closes the blinds before joining the kids in quiet, tense hiding. "Last year, I hid behind the teacher's metal desk," she recalls. "This year, I have tried out a few hiding places. Next time we have a drill we are supposed to hide in our cubbies where we put our backpacks. I think it is because we can't be seen if we hide in the cubby."

I asked her if she was scared during the drills. She looked up at me and said "No, why should I be scared?" It was then that her mom asked her if she knew why they were having lockdown drills. "Yes, we are practicing hiding."

Molly's mom, who was standing right next to her daughter, asked in a slightly anxious voice, "Who are you hiding from?"

The little girl stopped fidgeting with the toy she was playing with and looked up at her mom.

"I don't know for sure, but I think it is in case a bad person comes into the school to try and hurt me."

The mother looked like she was about to cry. I hoped that sweet child could not see my tears.

Molly saw her friend from across the street coming toward us and asked, "Can I go play now?"

While Molly, her mom, and I were speaking, her younger sister, Samantha, a kindergartener at the same school, had come to stand by us, listening to the conversation. She chimed in, "We have those drills, too. We have to hide. The teacher hides with us." She continued to share what happens in her class.

Molly and Samantha's mom then called for her husband to come join us. Mom asked if he knew that the girls had lockdown drills at school.

Dad answered a firm "No."

Mom asked the other parents standing nearby if they knew that their kids had lockdown drills during school. The parents all shook their heads in unison. "No."

Molly's friend Josh raised his hand as if to be called on in class. When I acknowledged him, he stated, "I get scared during the drills. But I try not to let anyone know it."

Josh's father's expression was one of pain and disbelief. He rubbed his son's head. "I had no idea the kids had these drills." He added that his son is only in first grade.

By now I had drawn a large gathering, as Josh's sisters—Logan (fourth grade) and Ellie (sixth grade)—eagerly joined the discussion. Logan stated that they have lots of drills at her school.

None of the parents were aware that the lockdown drills were happening at school. When they heard their children talking about lockdown drills, they started asking questions. One mom asked, "What happens if you are in the hallway during a drill?"

Logan and Ellie responded, "You have to go to the nearest classroom. If that door is locked, you knock. If no one answers you are supposed to run to the nearest bathroom, go in a stall, and put your feet on the toilet seat. Then no one will know you are there."

It took me several days to stop thinking about Josh, Logan, Ellie, and the sweet neighborhood kids who had shared their feelings about lockdown drills with me. I can't shake the vision of kids aged six, eight, and twelve standing on top of a toilet seat with the goal of hiding from a shooter. I am haunted by the reality that many caring, educated, and loving parents are not aware of this potentially traumatizing exercise.

I have always subscribed to the notion that knowledge is power and it's not any different in this situation. We are living in a new era where the realization is that neither the teacher nor the school principal can guarantee a child's safety. That is the complete opposite of what has been our assumption for years.

Middle-Schooler Kyle

During a conversation with Kyle, a quiet fourteen-year-old boy from a suburban town in New Jersey, I discovered that he spends a lot of time, and I mean *a lot of time*, playing video games on his devices. He admitted that he was addicted to gaming. He didn't think it was a bad thing. He said that he really enjoyed playing video games, as did his friends.

I asked him, if he was playing six to eight hours a day, then how did he have time to go outside?

"Outside?" he answered. "Why would I go outside?"

"To shoot basketball, ride a bike, or take your dog for a walk," I offered.

"I would never do that!" Now, he had my attention.

"Why not?" I asked. As Kyle listed his reasons for staying inside playing endless hours of violent video games, I heard something else. So I asked him, "Are you ever afraid to go outside?"

He turned his head as to not make eye contact with me, and said in a slight whisper, "Of course I am."

Here it is—another tragedy connected to the fear of gun violence; children are afraid to go outside of their homes to explore, hang out with friends, exercise, or just daydream.

"Kyle?" I asked. "What are you afraid will happen to you if you go outside?" I felt my body tense up as I braced for his answer.

He looked at me. "There are a lot of bad people in the world. I don't know if someone will try to abduct me, there are drive-by shootings, I might get hit by a drunk driver, or..." I missed the last few things he said because upon hearing just the first part of his answer, I was overwhelmed with sadness. This was not startling news to me. I have worked with children, teens, and their families for the last thirty years, but something has fundamentally changed.

Liam—A Junior in High School

Liam is a bright high school student who, in addition to tending to his studies, stays busy as a member of a political organization, a student leadership program, and other after-school activities. I met him on a rainy Sunday afternoon when his town's spring festival had to be moved indoors because of inclement weather. He and a few other student leaders were helping out at a drug and alcohol awareness table. I was struck by his ability to passionately connect with kids and adults who approached the table for pamphlets and information. At the conclusion of the program, I asked him if I could interview him for this book.

I asked him how he was doing with the lockdown drills at schools. "These drills have not affected me a lot because I have been acclimated to school shootings," he responded. "I remember that I was in middle school when the Sandy Hook Elementary School shooting happened. I've always had a fear that there will be a mass shooting at my school."

He added, "I remember crying when I learned about Sandy Hook. I was confused. My parents taught me that good things happen to good people, and bad things happen when people are bad. I was really naive when I was young. I just didn't get why this happened to little kids."

Liam told us that he learned about the Sandy Hook shooting online and on TV. "Actually, it was information overload—a lot for a kid." I asked if he remembered talking to his parents about the tragic event that impacted us all. He said "Yes." They promised him that they would keep him safe. A nervous laughter escaped his lips as looked away. "But I don't feel safe."

"When the Parkland shooting first started to be reported my phone lit up. I was in class. I got this sick feeling."

Liam poignantly commented, "I remember in the aftermath of the news coverage of Sandy Hook I saw parents break down outside the school. I couldn't comprehend what it must be like to experience that level of emotional pain. Too surreal."

I asked Liam how he learned about the mass school shooting in Parkland. He said, "I am a news junkie—I follow CNN, MSNBC. When the

Parkland shooting first started to be reported my phone lit up. I was in class. I got this sick feeling."

He told me how the young activists from Parkland High School continue to inspire him to speak out. He praised David Hogg, a Parkland student survivor, for urging other young people to not be afraid to feel their emotions and to dare to change the gun culture.

When I asked what were some of his fears regarding this subject he declared, "The scariest thing is that I fear that I am becoming desensitized to school shootings. I don't really get upset or fazed when there are lockdown drills or evacuation drills at school. I think that being in high school these days makes you numb to so many things."

Teens are naturally a complex mix of emotions, hormones, opinions, likes, and dislikes. Their moods can change faster than a Snapchat comment disappears, yet their honesty can cut through you. Liam was not much different than other teens I spoke with, although he was incredibly articulate. He had grown accustomed to having class interrupted by a lockdown or evacuation drill. He mostly expressed that these drills didn't scare him or his friends too much. Yet, on the other hand, he was quick to express that he expected his school to fall victim to a school shooting.

What Else Are Kids Saying?

Ross, an eleven-year-old boy who resides near Atlanta, Georgia, clearly told me that he does not feel anxious as a result of the lockdown drills he has in school. "I think we just have those drills a couple of times a year and they don't scare me." We continued to talk about his experiences during the drills, because I sensed that he might have wanted to express some other feelings. I asked him if he had a designated area to hide during the drills, or if he just chose a place himself.

"No, we just have to run really fast wherever we want to go. We are supposed to find a safe place to hide so no one can see us." He continued to tell me that the last time he hid, he went behind a part of the classroom wall that jutted out near the door because he didn't think a shooter in the hallway would be able to see him there.

I then asked him if he thought that his teacher got anxious or scared during the lockdown drills. He was quiet for a few seconds and then answered, "Yes." I asked him how he knew that. "I could tell by the look on her face," he responded. "She looked very scared and anxious."

I was struck by how insightful and attentive he was, but then I realized I shouldn't really be surprised. After all, we are teaching our children to literally run for their lives and hide from a potential shooter. Of course he had learned how to pay attention to the adults who are there to keep him alive. It was part of the survival techniques he had developed to cope with new stressors of school life.

Then, I asked him again if he was scared when hiding from a potential shooter. This time, he answered, "Yes!"

I think it is important that parents and teachers create a healthy space for children to express their fears and concerns. Despite all of those who have helped develop safe plans for our children, the kids still are forced to hide, and some are still dying. Let's not forget about how many teachers went into their careers because they love children. What would happen if part of the job description also stated that you are responsible for literally protecting your students' lives to the extent of potentially sacrificing your own?

I wonder what that would look like if it was written in a teacher's contract. Do you think we would actually pay our teachers more if this was part of their job?

Nothing Like Sisters

Sitting in the graceful family room, two sisters reluctantly agreed to speak with me. Alyssa, a head-turning seventeen-year-old, attends a large, regional high school, and her sister Dana just finished her freshmen year at a state university. The girls were cautious about talking to me at first, acting like the lockdown drills at their school never bothered them. At one point early on, Dana abruptly got up and said she was going to get a drink.

After she left, Alyssa explained that many "scary" things have happened at her school. She proceeded to tell me that one day earlier that year there was a man with a gun walking around the fields outside the building. "There was a lockdown drill, but many kids in my school didn't take it seriously," she said. "I started texting my mom, saying that something really strange was happening in the school." She added that her mom had received an alert that the school was in lockdown due to a potential shooter. "I was so freaked out. I was crying."

Alyssa's mom and dad decided to join us. Dad sat down next to his daughter on the couch, and Mom sat across from her family on a chair. Alyssa looked at her mom and said, "You don't know everything that happens in my school."

Alyssa told us about the last lockdown drill she experienced. "It didn't go so well. It was the first time we had a drill during lunchtime. There was something like 300 kids in the cafeteria when the announcement came over the PA system, but nobody seemed to care. Everyone was still talking. Some kids were joking around that it was a real shooting. The teachers and administrators could not get us quiet. We failed the drill, but nobody told us we failed. Later that day we had another lockdown and a lot of kids freaked out. Many of us thought it must be the real thing because we never have two drills in the same day."

She paused and looked at her mom and dad. "Like, we really freaked out. Some kids started crying and others were talking. It was so crazy that we failed that drill, too. What would have happened if there was a real shooter? We all would be dead!"

I looked at her parents' faces, and saw they were filled with fear and disbelief.

I asked Alyssa where she first learned about the shooting in Parkland. She said, "social media." She leaned in closer to me whispering, "I was at school."

We talked about how she felt when she heard about the school shooting. I looked directly at her dad as I asked her if she had talked to her parents about the shooting. "No," she answered. Dad shook his head no. I glanced over at mom as I asked her if she had talked to her mom about Parkland. "No," she answered. Alyssa looked at me. "I guess I should have talked to them about the shooting. It really freaked me out. I am still scared that something like that could happen at my school."

Two Track Stars

In another interview, Ellie and Stephanie spoke openly about what was on their minds as they concluded their sophomore and junior years, respectively. Ellie, a cross country and varsity runner, said that she mostly worried about getting good grades and getting into "a really good" college. Both girls stated that everyone is pretty stressed out about their grades, along with SAT and ACT scores.

When I asked the girls if they worried about being safe at school, it was as if I turned off the lights. The expressions on their faces went dim. They both looked down at the ground before looking at me again. Stephanie replied that everyone worried about the school getting shot up. "We have lockdown drills at least once a month," she said. "Someone is always posting about another school shooting on social media."

"Do you get scared during the drills?" I asked.

Stephanie answered, "Well, I try to act like it's no big deal. I listen to the drill and watch the teacher's face to see if they know if it is a drill or the real thing. The problem is, the school doesn't let the teachers know any more if it is a drill or the real thing." She paused. "I guess I get scared."

I asked, "Do you think your teacher gets nervous during the drills?"

Both girls nodded. "I know the teachers try to act like it is no big deal, but you can tell they are upset, annoyed, and even worried at times. Lately, the teachers tell us that we need to plan ahead by thinking about what items we can throw at the shooter. All we came up with is to throw our backpacks at a shooter, throw our sneakers, or something else handy. Most of our classes we do not use books anymore, so we don't have books to throw."

I asked them, "Do you talk to your parents about the lockdown and evacuation drills?"

Stephanie looked at me, shaking her head while answering, "No. My parents work a lot. I only see them for a few minutes late in the evening and we never talk about it."

I couldn't help it; my motherly advice slipped out. "It's totally under-standable to be scared during the lockdown drills. It's okay to be angry that you have to go through this exercise at least once a month. I am sorry, girls. I am sorry that schools are not making you feel safe."

Three Eighth Graders

I caught up with Corey, Andrew, and Paige at a street fair in their town. They seemed to be enjoying eating some of the local fare, fried dough on a stick. One of the boys' moms had volunteered them to speak with me. They had no idea what the topic was going to be.

I was excited to see that not one of the kids was staring at their phones. After we talked a bit about the best food to eat at the fair, I told them a little about the book I was writing. Silence followed. One of the boys looked away from me. The other pulled his phone out of his pocket and starting looking at it as if he had just received a text, but nothing was lit up.

However, the girl looked right at me, and she almost shouted her response, "Last week when we had a lockdown drill, our teacher told us to run and hide as fast as we could. I ran to the large garbage pail and crawled in it. I am pretty sure no one could see me from the pail. I didn't feel safe in there. I don't think the pail is bulletproof. I definitely will not hide in the garbage pail again."

"That must have been terrifying," I stated.

"Yup," she answered.

The three of them talked a bit more about their experiences. I thanked them and they rushed off to enjoy the delightful spring day. I felt guilty asking them to remember how scared they were when all they wanted was to hang out, enjoy life.

College Students Also Have Lockdown Drills

I find it interesting to watch people scroll endlessly on Snapchat or Instagram. They seem to become intoxicated right before your eyes. This is what was happening when I was sitting with Cara, a talkative college student at a small liberal arts college in a rural town. She told me that they don't really use the term "lockdown drills" in college.

"It works like this," she said. "You receive an alert on your phone." One day in the start of her freshmen year, she received such an alert stating that the entire campus was in lockdown, starting immediately. No one was to leave where they were. If they were outside, they were to enter the nearest building and go to a classroom, bathroom, or office. Cara told me she was in the library on campus hanging out with a few friends. "We were sitting by large windows overlooking the quad. We know we weren't supposed to move but we were scared being out in the open area of the library, especially because we were near the windows. We grabbed our stuff and ran to a quiet room. It had no windows. I was so grateful that I was with my friends."

Cara later learned that there had been a homicide about two miles from campus and the shooter was still on the run. According to the local paper, the university sent an Orange Alert to all students and repeated it for the next few hours. The alert let the community know that the police were investigating a crime off campus. It urged all students to remain indoors, not to let anyone in, and to shelter in place. Students who were in the library were asked not to leave. It took several hours till the incident was over.

Cara said, "I was terrified."

My Daughter's School, Too

My daughter attended a liberal arts college on the outskirts of Boston, located in a community that was known to be relatively safe. It was during this period that I learned about the bombing at the Boston Marathon on social media. I was checking my phone between client sessions when I saw the first horrific photos depicting some of the initial destruction. I quickly called my daughter to see if she had gone to watch the race as originally planned. No answer.

I called my husband—no answer. I waited. Finally, I received a text. "I am safe. Can't talk. I am okay. I am on campus. We are in a lockdown. Love you." The words beamed from my phone.

Breathe, breathe, I told myself. She is okay.

I talked to my daughter many times that day. The conversations included how upset, sad, and frightened she was. She had friends who were spectators, but all were safe. She let us know that she and her friends were staying on campus rather than a mile away at their rented house. But at some point, she and one of her roommates decided to make a run for it—literally. They left the library, ran to the parking lot, jumped into her car, and drove the mile to their house. She only told me she did this after they were home.

"Lock all the doors," I repeated in several texts.

To say that not many students or parents slept well that night is an understatement. Grandparents shared in the anxiety, too. It was my mother who texted my daughter, waking her up to say that the authorities had caught the bomber. The police found the bomber less than five miles from my daughter's house.

Stories like these, in some form or another, are happening in colleges and communities throughout our country.

Kids Are Sounding Hopeless

"It's been happening everywhere. I've always kind of felt like eventually it was going to happen here, too."[1]

---

[1] Charles M. Blow, "Enough Is Enough," *The New York Times*, May 20, 2018, https://www.nytimes.com/2018/05/20/opinion/santa-fe-school-shooting.html.

Many of the cable and public news stations played this clip, a prediction from a young female survivor of the May 18, 2018 Santa Fe High School shooting in Texas. The reporter seemed shocked by the child's honest answer. The newscasters sharing the report also seemed incredulous at the teen's statement.

I was not shocked. I was deeply saddened to hear her pessimistic view of growing up. In fact, I have been hearing this exact sentiment over and over again during my interviews with students. It has become commonplace for kids to feel a sense of not *if* but *when* a shooting will happen. Here is a compilation of some of what kids have shared with me:

"I know how to hide from a bad person if they come into my classroom. I am really smart."

"I am a good student because I know how to be quiet when told there is a dangerous threat to my life."

"I know what it feels like to sit quietly waiting to find out if a real shooter is in my school or if it is a drill."

"Guns kill innocent people. My mom worried when I used to walk to school. Now she drives me and picks me up every day."

"Mom and Dad worry when they drop me off at school. I know it, because you can see it in their faces."

"I don't tell my mom about the lockdown drills because she will worry too much."

"I have so much to worry about between getting good grades, making the sports teams, and getting into the best college that I don't have time to worry about being killed at school."

"I have friends who had friends killed in a school shooting."

"It is inevitable. There probably will be a shooting at my school."

"The adults in this country have lost control. Kids worrying about dying from gunshots is horrific and unacceptable."

"I worry that I will fall when I have to run in the dark to my hiding place. If I fall, it will take a few seconds for me to get back up, and in that time someone could come into my classroom and start shooting."

"The teacher says we should drop to the floor as soon as we get to our hiding space. We should stay away from the windows."

"I try to distract myself during a lockdown."

How Well Is Your Child Doing?

There are many variables to how "well" your child is handling this climate, including how the teacher prepares the students for the actual drills, how you have prepared your child, the culture in the school, your child's personality, and the home/community environment in which he or she is being raised.

It was extremely illuminating to speak to kids, some as young as four years old, others of elementary, middle school, high school, even college age, and ask them what they thought about experiencing lockdown drills in the era of school shootings.

Not only did their words educate me, they made me think about the things they didn't say, too. It was the looks they gave me and their whispers, letting me know how scared they really were at times. From the brave souls who disclosed their real-life nightmares of surviving the Parkland shooting, to my sweet neighbor Logan, there is no doubt in my mind that countless children are being traumatized.

Said one student, "My mom is so intense about saying goodbye to me in the morning before I leave for school. She hugs me and kisses me. She acts like this may be the last time she ever sees me. I tell her not to worry; I will be fine."

Sure, many kids put on a good face and seem to be adjusting to the current climate in their schools. The truth is, nobody knows the long-term consequences of being exposed to monthly school lockdown drills, along with all-too-many mass shootings.

I share these stories with you to let you know that your own children may be scared or just annoyed by the drills, but would really benefit from talking to you about their experiences. Parents need to be aware of the drills and what they are doing to their kids. Don't rely on my word; do your own research. Ask your kids how they feel during lockdown drills. Ask them how their friends feel about it. Then listen.

CHAPTER 3

What Parents and Teachers Are Saying and Doing

Reconnecting with an old camp friend is always fun, but this time my heart was breaking.

Randi was on her way to Target on the dreadful morning of February 14, 2018 in Parkland, Florida, to pick up some last-minute supplies for her daughter's sixteenth birthday. As she was driving, several unmarked police cars with their lights flashing went zooming by. When Randi came to a light, she texted her friend to see if she knew what was happening. The answer was no. At the next light, she texted her daughter, asking her if she was okay. "I had a bad feeling that something was going on at the school; all the cars were heading that direction," she told me.

By the time Randi parked her car in Target's parking lot she received a text: "Mom, we had a fire drill, but now we are having a Code Red." As Randi was walking into the entrance to Target, the next text read, "Mom, I am in the closet in the media room. This is the real thing. I love you. Tell everyone I love them."

"I just stood there, frozen," she said. "Until then, it just didn't compute. I just kept telling myself it would be okay—that we have had bomb scares before and it will probably be nothing." Another woman walking near her also stopped and stared at her phone. "We started to talk. 'What do we do? Should we drive over to the school?'"

Next came a call from her friend. "Can my son and his friend walk over to your house? They are reporting that two kids are dead and my son just got out." Randi's house is very close to the school campus.

Randi stated it was then that she and the stranger in the lobby starting crying, and others gathered as they tried to figure out what to do. Rumors were flying that shots were being fired through the windows, so they thought it best not to go to the school. They later learned that the gunman had been shooting through the glass windows of the doors into the classrooms.

One of the women standing in the lobby received a call from her husband. He had heard from the police that eight people were dead. Randi ran to the car and tried to get to the school.

Randi's daughter spent two and a half hours in the media closet with four staff members and fifty students. She was with a good friend, and the two students clung to each other the entire time.

Eventually, a SWAT team came to the media room and released the kids who were told to leave the building quickly. The kids were only permitted to exit the campus in one direction—and it turned out to be in the direction of the local synagogue. Eventually, Randi's husband was able to meet up with their daughter there.

What Parents Are Saying

Many parents with whom I have spoken keep their worries about school violence at the forefront of their minds, while others tuck them away. I try to learn what they specifically worry about, how they talk to their kids about violence, and even how they think their kids are doing in this current climate of fear of being shot in school.

Many parents who agreed to talk greeted me with slight apprehension, some with annoyance, others with a look of fear and trepidation when I said: "I am writing a book on the challenges of raising your children in a climate of fear. How do you feel about your kids having to experience lockdown drills in school?"

An alarming number of these parents had no idea that their children were experiencing lockdown drills at school. Many didn't understand the specifics of lockdowns and were not aware of the monthly exercise of students hiding under desks and in closets, huddling together as they waited to find out if the drill was the "real" thing. I discovered that many schools did not alert parents to the fact that a drill was going to be held on a specific day. It was the rare school that emailed the parents letting them know about the drill.

After hearing his kids talk to me about the drills, a father of four elementary school children declared, "I am shocked. I had absolutely no idea that my kids were hiding under desks, in supply closets, and standing on toilets, all in an attempt to hide from a crazy person."

One mother of two preschoolers described how her kids had "quiet time" drills once a month in their private school. She said that her daughter tells her that everyone knows that you *must* be quiet during the drills. Mom added that it broke her heart to think that the little ones had to experience such drills. Although she knew they didn't really understand why they had to be quiet, it was still very upsetting.

Other parents told me, "I didn't know that it happened every month."

"I really have no idea what my kid does during a lockdown drill."

Some parents answered, "No, my kids are fine. They have been having lockdown drills just like they've had fire drills since they were little."

I have heard many comments such as, "I really have no idea what my kid does during a lockdown drill. I am sure they are fine or I would have heard about it."

After I have the opportunity to explain to parents that a lockdown drill, active shooter drill, or some other type of drill typically occurs once a month, I usually get a reaction of surprise that the drills happen so often. However, once parents engage in conversation about the drills, they start to understand the reality of what is going on.

"I need to ask my kid about the drills," some parents tell me. "We never talk about it. I don't think it bothers him." Other parents look at me quizzically and ask, "I guess I should talk to them about the drills?"

"I did not know that my child was hiding in a closet," disclosed one mom. Another added, "I have never asked my child about the lockdown or evacuation drills. I wonder if they upset her."

A father stated that he figured if his kids were upset by the drills, they would have come to talk to him. I encouraged this dad to reach out to his kids and attempt to engage them in conversation.

Bathrooms Are Scary Places

I sat down with Rachel, a mom of two children in elementary school. She had learned about my book through a mutual friend. In a concerned voice, she said that she had been contemplating what to do about this situation. She said, "I talk to my girls about pretty much everything that has to do with staying safe, not talking to strangers . . . you name it, we talk about it. My girls tell me when there is a lockdown drill or an evacuation drill. I even know where they hid that day and how they felt. My daughter, Madison, is eleven years old but going on fifteen, you know what I mean?

"Recently, I noticed that every day when I went to pick up my daughters from school, Madison asked me to wait while she went to the bathroom. The other day, half joking, I asked her if she was allowed to go to the bathroom during the day. I was trying to figure out what was going on. Madison answered, 'Yes, but I don't go.'"

Her daughter said that she was scared to go to the bathroom during the day because of what the principal told them: If someone is in the hallway during a lockdown drill they have to run to the nearest classroom. "If we are in the bathroom, we have to make sure to put our feet on the seat and stay very quiet," Madison told her mother. "If I was going to hide and maybe even die, I just don't want to be in the bathroom."

Rachel asked me if she should email the teacher and let her know how her daughter was feeling. I urged her to speak with the teacher, principal, and other people in authority about her concerns. I hope the staff help the children handle their stress. Perhaps they could try the buddy system, letting kids go in pairs to the bathroom.

Just think for a moment the amount of stress and anguish that Madison feels worrying about going to the bathroom at school. Unfortunately, I have heard many forms of this story from parents and kids.

Looking for Guidance

During a parenting forum at which I was the keynote speaker, a mother of a five-year-old asked me for some guidance. She said that in trying to discuss the lockdown drills with her son, she thinks she scared him. This is a typical problem that parents run into. Giving too much information overwhelms the child, often causing unnecessary fear.

Another parent joined the conversation, stating that she had just moved to this country and was now having second thoughts. She said that she had no idea that there were lockdown drills and so many school shootings. She wants to pack up her bags and move back to her home country where guns are not allowed.

Many parents expressed a sense of helplessness about the current state of affairs. They hate that their children are forced to play "hide and seek" from a potential shooter, although they understand the need for these exercises.

"I worry all the time about school shootings," said one parent. "I tell my daughter to never go anywhere without her phone. I also demand that she text me back immediately after I text her." This mom continued to say that one day when her daughter was not responding to her texts, she got so concerned she called the school to see if everything was okay in the school.

A mom of four children living in a city that is ranked high in crime told me, "Sometimes I don't know if I worry more about my kids getting shot on the way to school or in the school." She continued, "I make sure to talk to my kids about how to walk so you don't get noticed. We talk about how to hide in the bathroom, whether it is from another student with a gun or knife, or from an outsider with a gun. They know that if you are near a bathroom, you make a run for the bathroom stall, crouch on the toilet seat, and make sure your head doesn't appear over the top of the stall door. One of my boys is very tall. I tell him he has to make sure he squats down."

I heard from many parents of boys that they were very concerned about their child's obsession with playing violent video games. Many concurred that their child's endless hours of gaming bothered them prior to the latest school shooting, but now they worry there is a correlation.

Numerous parents stated that their boys insisted that the most popular video game called *Fortnite* was not violent because it was not bloody. It is important to note that the game is primarily about shooting and killing and is full of bullets, guns, and grenades, but it doesn't show blood after a character is killed. Have we as a society decided something is only considered violent when there is blood? (You can read more about *Fortnite* and other disturbing video games in Chapter 4, "Virtual Violence: Is It Really Bad?")

One mother told me that she calls the parents of her child's friends before she allows her to go over to their homes. She stated that she asks if they have guns in the home. If they are gun owners, her child is not permitted to visit.

A Son Shares His Feelings

During a fortunate encounter with a mom and her children in line for the dressing room at Target, I asked the mom if I could speak with her kids. Her two younger children, a boy age eleven and girl age nine eyed me suspiciously as my twentysomething daughter rolled her eyes and walked away.

This mom didn't seem particularly interested in my questioning until her son said that sometimes he hides in the supply closet for over twenty minutes. He said he doesn't get too upset, but a few of the other kids do. He looked up at his mom and said, "Yesterday, Jessica started crying while we were hiding." I asked him what happened next. He said that another girl held her hand and the teacher hugged her.

Mom then launched into active listening mode. When I finished all my questions, she grabbed her son and hugged him tightly stating, "I had no idea, I had no idea."

When her sixteen-year-old daughter walked up and joined us, she asked what was going on. The boy retold his story of how some of the girls in his class get really upset during lockdown drills, but he is fine.

The son seemed empowered by his latest experience of telling a stranger and his mom his experiences. Did he feel safer by sharing the experiences? Did he feel more understood, and therefore, more connected to his mom?

When I asked the mother if I could speak to her children about the topic of lockdown drills, I helped her to stop rushing through her errands and focus on her children. Together, the mom and I acknowledged her kids' experiences and validated their feelings. This is one the most significant things a parent can do for a child. It helps them build a solid foundation while allowing them to feel safe.

His older sister said, "Yeah, we have lots of lockdown drills at school." As she continued her story, my eyes were glued to the mom. By now, she was holding her younger two children close to her, staring intently at her daughter as she spoke.

The mom reached her arms out to me, bringing me close in a warm hug, all the while thanking me for helping her pay attention.

"Good luck on your book," said the boy as I walked away in search of my daughter.

Of course, there are parents on the other side of the spectrum, too. But the majority of those I spoke with, although they seemed to be well intended, were overprotective. Although many were dedicated to running their children's schedules, they did not seem to have lockdown drills on their radar.

For example, Amanda, a full-time working mom of three teens, wouldn't even let me finish my question about lockdown drills. "Of course, I talk to my kids," she said. "We talk about the drills the day they happen.

They tell me where they were hiding, along with lots of details about how long they were hiding, what the teacher did, and so forth. I can't imagine how they would deal with the stress if we didn't talk about it."

A Fifth Grader's Perspective

I was sitting with Jack, a fifth grader, and his mom in their comfortable living room. Jack was leaning against his mom, flipping through his younger cousin's storybook as we talked about school lockdown drills. He answered my questions in a matter-of-fact manner until I asked him if he ever became frightened during the drills. Jack quickly sat up, dropping the book as he turned to his mom. "Remember, Mom, when there was that 'problem' outside of my school?" He told me that he could see from his classroom window that a girl had driven her car onto the field. She got out of the car, carrying a gun and was screaming. "Remember, Mom?" he said again.

Jack's mom reassured him that the police had come to school quickly and everyone stayed safe while in their lockdown drills. Jack wanted me to know it was really scary. "I think about that sometimes during the drills and wonder what would have happened if she had come into my school."

After the interview, Jack's mother let me know that she was grateful for speaking with Jack. She was not aware of how concerned he was about school shootings.

Reactions to Parkland

In the immediate weeks after the Parkland school shooting, parents' and children's anxiety peaked. Numerous administrators and teachers told me they received many emails and calls from concerned parents inquiring about school safety. Many districts increased police protection in and around schools.

During a drug/alcohol and mental health task force committee meeting in my town, several parents stated their concern for their children's safety. Many parents offered school safety suggestions. Some wanted police officers stationed at every door and metal detectors in the main entrance of the high school, while others focused on getting involved in community organizations to advocate stronger gun laws.

My research revealed that several schools in New Jersey enforced new policies limiting the number of adults going in and out of the buildings. The new policy prohibited parents and caregivers from dropping off their child's forgotten homework assignments, athletic gear, and lunches. If a child did not come to school with all their supplies, they would have to do without for the day. The school would lend them money to buy lunch. The hope was that this policy would permit the school to better monitor every person going in and out of the building.

Many school boards continue to debate the best policies for keeping students and staff safe. In some communities, parents are leading the discussion by pushing school boards to debate complicated issues of physical safety. I encourage all school districts, superintendents, and school boards to include how this climate of fear is affecting our children's mental health in their discussions.

I did not find one school, private or public, that has a policy to notify parents that a lockdown drill occurred during the school day.

What Teachers Are Saying

I have spoken to a large number of teachers about their thoughts on gun violence and lockdown drills, and in particular, how the atmosphere in their schools has changed as more incidents have taken place across the country.

A Threat and Mistaken Identity

I asked Missy, a soft-spoken young teacher who was clearly older than she looked, how her students reacted after the school shooting in Parkland.

She told me that on February 22, 2018, eight days after the Parkland shooting, someone posted on Snapchat their intent to shoot up a school that happened to have the same initials as her's. The post went viral very quickly, and after a parent reported the threat, police showed up at her high school at 7:45 a.m.

The Snapchat post read, "Attention BHS students: Prepare to see my wrath tomorrow…I am going to be the next to go down in history. I dare you to go to school tomorrow. I want to see how many people I can take with me."

Police and school administrators determined it was a prank, but at that point many students had texted their parents saying they were in lockdown. At least 500 parents showed up to the school to pick up their kids, creating a hectic situation for school officials.[1]

Upon researching this incident, I learned that a student from New Mexico had created a secondary Snapchat account. He shared it with a few other people, and before long, it went viral. It's scary how simple it was. Some of the reports indicated that kids were texting their parents that morning from school, saying that they were in lockdown in their classes.

Meanwhile, two other schools in the country, one in Texas, also iden-tify by the same initials as Missy's school. They all thought that a crazy shooter had targeted *their* school.

Missy stated that many students and parents were rattled by the threat, and that many kids were not in school the following day. Stu-dents discussed how scary the whole incident was and wondered if such a thing could happen there.

Vague Procedures and Confusion

Lauren is a relatively new middle school teacher in a well-to-do sub-urb. When I asked what her school administration instructed her to do during lockdowns and other drills, her answer surprised me. She

---

[1] Corey W. McDonald, "Threat Against 'BHS Students' Causes Panic in Bayonne," NJ.com, February 24, 2018, https://www.nj.com/jjournal-news/index.ssf/2018/02/threat_against_bhs_students_ca.html.

recalled at the beginning of the school year, the principal went over the procedures of all the different drills, including lockdown, fire, and shelter in place. She said the only other time they discussed the drills was at the end of the year. "Even after the shooting in Parkland, there was no discussion or special meeting about what happened, how to answer kids' potential questions; nothing to help address the students' fear," she confided.

I asked her if she noticed any changes in her students after the shooting in Parkland. "Yes. We had a lockdown drill two days afterward. You could just tell that the students were distressed by the drill. Some of the kids asked me, 'Are you sure this is just a drill?' Honestly, it was a bit scary for me, too!"

"Aren't we just making it easier for the shooter to kill more of us?'"

She continued: "Our school did implement some new procedures after Parkland. We now have little shades over the classroom door windows. When we have a lockdown drill, I lock the door and then pull down the shade. However, we no longer pull down the blinds on the classroom windows to the outside. Apparently, there are numbers on the windows in case police need to identify our classroom. It is really confusing. One of the questions the kids ask me now is, 'Why do we have to turn the lights off when we are keeping the blinds up?'

"Other questions I hear from my students are, 'How do we know if it is really a drill?' and, 'Why do we sit all together in a corner of the room? Aren't we just making it easier for the shooter to kill more of us?'"

Lauren said she thought a lot about the threat of school violence. "I did some research this year on school shootings," she told me. "Some of the latest says that teachers and students should throw things at a shooter. The idea is that if you throw a printer, tennis balls, books, it could make the shooter miss his target as he is shooting." She paused for a few seconds. "I don't know if that would really work."

Lauren felt that her principal was very vague when it came to talking directly about the procedures of a lockdown drill. "After we lock doors, pull the shade, and turn off lights, we were told to 'think on our feet.'" She remembers the principal adding, "Do whatever you have to do as a good human being."

Lauren related that most of the kids try to act like tough guys and that the drills are no big deal, but you can tell it upsets some of them. She said she was so grateful that at least in her school they are always told that it is a drill.

Baseball Bats, Tennis Balls, and Rocks

Lena, a seasoned high school teacher, admitted that she keeps a baseball bat next to her classroom door, just in case. I asked, "Just in case?"

She answered, "Yes, just in case a shooter or another dangerous person enters the classroom, I have the bat. I can't imagine not being able to do something to try and protect my students."

I asked her if any of the kids have asked why she has a bat by the door. She said that she explained to them why it is there. "I think it makes them feel safer." I wonder if it really does make Lena's students feel safer.

Lena continued to tell me that it is a new trend in her school now. No one says it directly, but she knows many teachers who keep things in the classroom. I have heard of people keeping a golf club within reach. Someone has a bag of rocks. Another teacher keeps a basket of tennis balls. They all have the same idea. If an intruder entered the class, the students would have some things to throw. Hopefully, they would be able to knock the person down, or at least knock the gun out of his or her hands.

I asked Lena if she became anxious or scared during the drills. She responded, "Well, I am not happy about them. I know what I have to do, but I do worry. It is a really big deal if a teacher forgets to lock the classroom door. I worry that I would forget. I worry that I wouldn't be able to protect my kids. I worry what would happen to my own kids if something happened to me."

Lena stated that she knows of teachers who identify the two biggest guys in each of their classes and pull them aside. The teacher instructs them that if there ever is a situation with a shooter, they should plan on jumping on him while the teacher and the students try to hit him with the bat kept next to the door.

Putting Lives on the Line

Cassie, one of my childhood friends and a fourth-grade teacher in a mostly Latino urban school district, explained to me how challenging it is to communicate with parents about many issues including school safety. She tells her students that it is her job to keep them safe during lockdowns. She told me that her students handle the drills very well— even her most challenging kids get it. They are able to pull it together and behave appropriately. She believes her students cooperate because of how she introduces the idea of the drills at the beginning of the year. "I tell them, 'This is the deal: We have these drills in order to keep you all safe. It is my job to keep you safe. I will do whatever I have to do to keep my word.' I also tell them to tell their parents that their teacher will keep them safe."

She said that even though she has two children, she knows that if anything ever happened in her school, she would put herself between the shooter and the kids. "How crazy is that?"

The interview with Cassie demonstrates that something is terribly wrong in American schools if teachers have to consider putting their lives on the line when they sign up for the job.

Images of Cassie and me running through the woods behind her house came rushing back. She always was the brave one, the first to jump over the stream or climb across the water on a skinny log. The way I see it, her bravery is called into practice every day now.

A Foundation of Trust

"I have an uneasy feeling almost every time I say goodbye to my child in the morning. I make a point of saying 'I love you,'" states Kira, a middle school counselor. "I make sure that my husband, my daughter, and I all connect before we leave the house. I work in a school, my daughter goes to school, and the risks exist."

The school counselor said that it is her job to help parents develop a trusting relationship not only with her, but with teachers and the school. "I feel it is critical that the parents trust us." She continued to explain that having a foundation of trust permits her to help the parents help their children. She described her surprise at how often she needs to encourage parents to have honest conversations with their kids, especially about tough subjects. She emphasizes the need for parents to share with the school when the child and/or family is experiencing a trauma or change, such as a death in the family, or a divorce.

"It equips us to better attend to the child's individual needs," she said. "We have been seeing a rise in anxiety across the board. It still seems like mental health issues are a stigma. Many parents are uncomfortable talking to us about their child's issues." This becomes particularly challenging when working with families from various cultural backgrounds.

During an interview with Brett, a high school health teacher, I learned that his manner of preparing his students about the current risks actually included citing survival statistics, which I thought could be extremely jarring. At one point in our interview, I couldn't help but interrupt him. "What do these kids say when you tell them the percentage of their chance of survival?" Brett didn't answer me. He just continued to tell me that the big windows in the school auditorium had been replaced with bullet-proof glass, and that the school now had three armed police guards.

I'm afraid this story illustrates the mass chaos that is the norm in our country. There is no "right" way to hold lockdown drills. School boards and administrators continue to search for the best ways to keep children safe. The problem here is that Brett is raising the level of anxiety in at least a few of his students. My suggestion to Brett would be to say, "We have a new policy this year. During lockdown drills we are no longer going to all hide together in a big group. Instead, break up into smaller groups and find hiding places."

There is no need for numbers of how many kids can die, will die, or have died. They are smart. They know that if a person with a gun enters their classroom it is not good.

A School Administrator Devises Strategies

Dr. Eli Warren, a school administrator, said it is very stressful preparing for lockdown drills, and that all teachers and staff need to review their roles in them. In his school, every teacher carries a key to their classroom doors around their necks, along with their identity cards. As soon as the drill is announced, the teacher locks the door with the key and then pulls down the window shade. Dr. Warren said that their biggest issue is that some teachers forget to lock the doors. After the drill, the administrator meets with any such teacher to devise strategies in order to help them remember to perform that vital action.

Are Teachers Superheroes?

Schools expect their teachers to become superheroes—have we gone too far?

On July 13, 2018, Madison Township, Ohio, held an emergency board of education meeting to discuss their recent recommendation that teachers should carry guns. Teachers could take a three-day training to permit them to have guns on school property.

I did not locate any policy regarding *where* teachers of that township were going to store their guns while they were in school. However, arming teachers is never a good idea. As this debate plays out in Madison Township, Ohio, it is doing the same in small towns and cities throughout our country.

This continues to be a deeply passionate argument in Madison township due to the fact that on February 29, 2016, there was a shooting at the high school. Two students were shot, but fortunately survived. What if teachers had been carrying guns that day? What if they had additional security guards carrying guns? Would more children and teachers have been shot or killed? Crossfire is a real risk.

I agree with student Eva Adams, a survivor of the 2016 Madison Township school shooting. "If teachers wanted to be police people, they would have been have become police officers."[2]

What Should Parents Do?

How can you help your children and their teachers negotiate these tough times of lockdown drills and gun violence in school? How closely can you watch and direct your children, and at what point does parental oversight become too much—counterproductive, even—despite the gravity of the situation?

Many of us are familiar with the term *helicopter parent,* coined in 1990 by Jim Fay, a parenting and educational consultant, and psychiatrist Foster W. Cline, MD, in their book, *Parenting with Love and Logic: Teaching Children Responsibility.*[3]

Julie Lythcott-Haims, author of the book, *How to Raise an Adult: Break Free of the Overparenting Trap and Prepare Your Kid for Success,* argues that "overparenting" is doing more harm than good as it "robs them of the chance to learn who they are, what they love, and how to navigate the world." She further writes, "We want so badly to help them by

[2] Zilka, Ashley, "Madison School Shooting Shaped—and Split—Community's Views on Guns in Schools," WCPO television news report, July 13, 2018, https://www.wcpo.com/news/local-news/butler-county/madison-township/madison-school-shooting-shaped-and-split-community-s-views-on-guns-in-schools.

[3] Foster Cline and Jim Fay, *Parenting With Love and Logic Teaching Children Responsibility,* (Colorado Springs, Colo: Pinon Press, 1990).

shepherding them from milestone to milestone, and by shielding them from failure and pain. But over-helping causes harm. It can leave young adults without the strengths of skill, will, and character that are needed to know themselves and to craft a life."[4]

Lythcott-Haims lists cultural events or shifts that led to helicoptering behaviors:

+ The 1981 abduction of Adam Walsh led to *America's Most Wanted* and photos of missing children on milk boxes

+ The self-esteem movement

+ The parent-joined play date

Basically, parents started worrying that their child may end up on the milk box, so their parenting style changed. They started keeping kids at home or at supervised playdates.

Psychoanalyst Erik Erikson noted that this is also antithetical to the needs of a developing adolescent. Through this period of storm and stress, "If an adolescent fails to work on one's own identity formation, it would result in role diffusion, alienation, and a lasting sense of isolation and confusion."[5]

Research has continued to prove that these intense parenting styles are harming our children. In a 2016 issue of the *Journal of Child and Family Studies*, Kayla Reed and other researchers noted that children with helicopter parents showed low levels of self-efficacy and the ability to handle some tougher life tasks and decisions. As a result, they had higher levels of anxiety and depression.[6]

One of my favorite parenting "gurus" is Wendy Mogel, a clinical psychologist and author of many books that explore how helicopter parents

---

[4] Julie Lythcott-Haims, *How to Raise an Adult: Break Free of the Overparenting Trap and Prepare Your Kid for Success* (New York: St. Martin's Press, 2015).

[5] Scott White, "Blocking Bulldozers," National Association of College Admission Counseling, https://www.nacacnet.org/news—publications/publications/journal-of-college-admission/blocking-bulldozers/.

[6] "Helicopter parents: Hovering May Have Effect as Kids Transition to Adulthood," Florida State University, June 26, 2016, https://www.sciencedaily.com/releases/2016/06/160628110215.htm.

often stunt their child's ability to launch into adulthood by their over-protectiveness, or even their inability and refusal to let them struggle and fail on their own.

Mogel shares a story of how a college admissions counselor described some freshmen students as "tea cups" because of how fragile they are when they get to college. She continued the story by describing how a kid went to the salad bar at the dining hall and called his mom asking if he likes Russian dressing. The child couldn't remember if he liked Russian dressing, or perhaps decided it was easier and less of a risk if he just called his mom and asked her.

I found this story to be extremely poignant and have shared it many times at parenting workshops, always giving Mogel credit, of course. I can see by the parents' reactions who is struggling with being hyper-involved in their child's life without setting some really good boundaries. Sometimes, I even have to explain to parents the meaning of Mogel's story.

It is only in recent years that children have the opportunity to text or call their parents the very instant they feel discomfort or anxiety. What would this young man have done if he didn't have a phone in his hand? He would have tried Russian dressing to determine if he liked it, or he may have taken the safe route and just had oil and vinegar. The point is that this pattern of co-dependence between the child and the parent started a long time before the kid was dropped off at school.

This again shows how important it is that you proactively communicate with your kids about their experiences, and I give specific tips for that in Chapter 5, "Talking to Your Kids About Violence."

How Kids React to Your Oversight

You may get anxious about whether your daughter turned in her math homework or how your son did on his history test, but please don't text your kids during the school day! It not only interrupts their focus, but also distracts them from their studies and often floods them with uncomfortable thoughts. One child stated, "I feel so bad my mom is worried. She wouldn't be able to handle it if something happened to me."

You are not the only parent who texts their kids during the school day.

My interviews revealed that parents are texting their kids too frequently, asking them simple logistical questions in an effort to stay connected, to keep track of them, and sometimes simply because it makes them feel needed. Some parents have gone to great lengths like installing extra tracking apps on their kids' phones. I have parents telling me they "need" to know where their kids are at all times. They even know when they are in lunch, gym, or history class.

Kids have revealed to me that their parents text them too often during the school day and get angry if they don't respond immediately. One kid stated, "Mom, I am in class. I can't just text you all the time." He added, "She does not think that is an acceptable excuse." Other responses included:

"If my mom is so worried all the time, there probably is a good chance something bad is going to happen to me."

"My mom doesn't have faith in me that I can handle myself if and when there is a real emergency."

"I need my parents to help me problem-solve difficult situations."

"I freak out when I cannot connect when I want to with my parents."

When Your Child Asks for Help

Parents say that they don't always know what to do when their kids come to them for help. I called the chief of police in a small community and I asked him how his school district handled lockdown drills. He said that his son's high school had recently implemented a phone app called Say Something Anonymous Reporting System. This was created by some parents from Sandy Hook after its tragedy. The chief recounted how his son had mentioned that he was grateful that such a system was now in place. He told me, "I am hopeful that this app will serve many purposes for both students and parents. I hope that it allows children to feel that what they see or feel is not only significant, but valued. In addition, it can help everyone feel that they are part of the community, and together they can work toward the common goal of keeping everyone safe."

Find out if your community has a program like this in place. If not, start advocating for it with your school administration to get an anonymous reporting program installed.

Several years ago, the community in which I raised my daughters tragically lost three teens in six months to suicide. In one school year, two high school graduates and one senior all killed themselves. I quickly put together a group for parents to learn and discuss strategies for talking with their kids. I can't forget a mom sitting in the front row of the crowded library auditorium. She raised her hand to answer a question, but it quickly turned into her confession of guilt.

The only thing that is not okay to do is to do nothing!

Her daughter had come to her before the latest suicide, informing her that there was this kid posting terrible things on his Snapchat and Instagram accounts. "She even showed me some of his disturbing comments," the mom said as tears streamed down her face. "*I didn't do anything!* I looked at the photos, I read this child's plea for help, and I did nothing. The next morning my daughter told me he was gone—he did it. He killed himself. I let my daughter down. I could have saved someone's child. I did nothing."

Reinforce to your kids that if they are concerned about a fellow classmate it is okay to tell you, a teacher, their guidance counselor, a trusted adult, or even make an anonymous phone call to the school principal or nurse. When your child comes to you with something that is upsetting them, maybe a text message from an angry friend or shares with you a disturbing photo from someone's Snapchat thread, listen to them. It isn't easy for many to come to you for help. Here's what you can do:

- **If your child comes to you for help, jump into action.** Acknowledge how hard it must have been for them to come to you. Validate the effort, but don't launch into "fix it" mode. Talk about various options for what they could do. The exception to this would be if the issue has to do with a potential suicide or plan to hurt others, in which case you should take action immediately.

- **Think about what you would want another parent to do.** If another parent knew your child was vaping weed, engaging in some other illegal or dangerous activity, would you want them to contact you? It may be a difficult phone call to make, but in the end, you are acting in a responsible manner while teaching your child what it means to live in a community.

- **Be present.** If your child is sneaking around, try to figure out why. "I noticed that you often come in from school and run with your backpack right upstairs to your room. I feel like you may be trying to hide something from me." Watch for their reaction. Do they get angry, secretive, storm away? Yes, I know they are teens, but still they're telling you something.

- **Talk before snooping.** To snoop or not to snoop? If your gut tells you to, do it. The first step is always to try to talk with your child to get them to tell you what is going on. Set up a contract with your child about screen usage and social media. Just like you need to know your child's passwords, you should know what social media apps they use. Sit down with your child once a week to go over who has sent them a friend request and discuss it. A psychotherapist reported that she does this with her thirteen-year-old daughter. She asks her daughter if she knows the person who sent her a friend request. "Mom, it is my friend Kelly's good friend Denise."

Mom asks, "Do you know Denise; have your ever met her? How do you know that it isn't an old man or some other person pretending to be another teen?" Have a healthy conversation with your child about who they accept. If that doesn't work, snoop. It is your home. More than likely, you purchased your child's phone for them and you pay for the internet service. It is your job to keep your child safe. Many, many times I have had teens tell me, or even tell their parents while in my office, how grateful they are that their parents helped them.

+ **Worry about one of their friends.** I always recommend telling your child if you are concerned about one of his or her friends. For example, "How's Sammy? He seems really sad lately. He doesn't seem okay. His eyes are always red when he comes over and he won't make eye contact with us. Do you think he is okay?" Pause. Let there be silence. Some kids may storm out only to revisit the subject at another time. By having this conversation you are letting your child know you are present and that you pay attention to them and their friends. If you are concerned about Sammy, you might say, "I am really worried about him. I am going to call his parents. I am not asking you if it is okay; I am just letting you know I am doing it. I don't want you to be surprised if Sammy tells you that I called."

+ **Remember you are not your kid's best friend.** Taking a strong stance helps your child feel safe. Remember, it is this sense of safety that helps them navigate through the tough stuff like school lockdown drills.

Sometimes, moms and dads tell me that they don't want to betray their child's trust so they don't reach out to other parents. However, you can make an anonymous phone call to the school. Leave a message for the school crisis counselor or principal.

The key is to include your children in the conversation. In Chapter 5, "Talking to Your Kids About Violence," I provide much more detailed guidance for this.

What Can Teachers Do?

Teachers are obviously a critical factor in managing students' anxiety level during lockdown drills. Robin, a veteran high school teacher in an urban area, stated that her school's lockdown drills include the typical protocol: Make sure that any kids in the hallway are shuttled into your classroom, lock the door, turn off the lights, and get all the kids to the back of the room. What is different in her school is that they have to take a sticker off the door window. (The removal of the sticker lets the authorities know that there are people in this classroom.)

This was a step I had not heard before. Why the sticker? In case of a school shooting, will this help the police and paramedics to avoid wasting time by going into an empty classroom, or will it tip off shooters as to where to find students?

Robin explained that compliance is key for all drills, from lockdowns to evacuations to shelter in place. If the teachers don't encourage the students to follow directions, it can become a very challenging situation.

When asked if her students find the drills upsetting, she said, "No. I know my kids. If I have a student who is flipping out or tends to be very sensitive, I will seek them out and try to comfort them."

Robin admits that her family worries about her safety. They bring it up often. "I don't worry, but it is on my mind at times. There are teachers who are very concerned that our school could be next." Then she added, "I think it is an absurd idea for teachers to carry guns."

Useful Tools to Keep Kids as Well-Adjusted as Possible

Here are some guidelines to keep kids as well-adjusted as possible in these difficult situations.

Preschool and Elementary Children

+ Prepare your students ahead of time for what a drill will be like.

+ Even if the students participated in drills the year before, repeat the procedure. Tell them you are there to keep them safe.

+ Remind them that the principal, other teachers, and police officers are all there to protect them.

+ State that millions of students just like them go to school every day and are safe.

+ Give them a chance to ask questions.

+ Keep a few picture books in certain areas of the room where you and the students hide. During a drill, hold up a book and pretend you are reading them a story. Let the children look at the pictures and create a story in their head. This can serve as a good distraction.

+ Teach your students how to do simple meditation and mindful breathing techniques. For more on this, see Chapter 6, "Strategies to Help Your Child (and You) Cope."

+ Teach your students a few basic sitting yoga poses such as a tree pose, which is an introductory balancing pose that just about all body abilities can enjoy. Tell your students to start by placing one heel on the side of their other ankle. As balancing progresses, the foot can be placed on the calf or thigh. However, make sure to avoid any pressure on the knee joint. The hands press together at midline, palm to palm, providing additional stability. Take several deep breaths as you hold the pose.

+ Assume the "cat pose." Start on your hands and knees in a "tabletop" position. Make sure your knees are set directly below your hips and your wrists and that elbows and shoulders are in line and perpendicular to the floor. Center your head in a neutral position, eyes looking at the floor. As you exhale, round your spine toward the ceiling, making sure to keep your shoulders and knees in position. Release your head toward the floor, but don't force your chin to your chest. Inhale, coming back to neutral "tabletop" position on your hands and knees.

+ Play a sitting version of Simon Says. Tell the kids that you will play a silent version of Simon Says where you are Simon.
    —Touch your shoulders
    —Touch your feet
    —Touch your head, etc.

After the drill is over, provide your students with a chance to recover. Tell them that their brain needs a chance to release all the excess energy that was created. You know your kids and whether or not it's appropriate to let them skip around the room for two minutes. Have them do jumping jacks, or run in place. Then have them do some body stretches, allowing their breath to go in and out. End with several deep breaths and releases. This will be good for you and your students; it respects that the drill was a stressful interruption, but they successfully navigated it.

Middle School and High School Students

+ Use a variation of the list for preschool and elementary school students, modified for age appropriateness.

+ Allow students to talk about how the drills affect them.

+ Provide some time for them to readjust to focusing on classwork.

+ Remember that students often act as if the drills are no big deal, but they may be just pretending.

+ Request that your school administration provide additional resources, and talk about their own experiences in this era of school violence.

+ Create a two-minute pause after the drill is over for the students to reset. Try the yoga poses listed earlier.

Creating Comfort

The majority of America's school children are safe at school, but they are being negatively affected by lockdown drills and by not having a safe place to talk about their experiences. Based on my many interviews for this book, countless kind, loving, and involved parents just don't seem to be familiar with what is really happening to their children during lockdown procedures.

The bottom line is that you must appreciate the extraordinary stress teachers experience from these drills, not to mention that from the possible threat of a school intruder. School boards, school administrators, teachers, and parents need to communicate a cohesive message to children: They are safe!

As Dr. Elana Zion, a child and adolescent psychiatrist and mother, stated, "I am very concerned about the mental well-being of many children today. Many of my colleagues agree that there is a significant rise in childhood and adolescent anxiety and depression." I asked Dr. Zion if her clients talk about school shootings and lockdown drills. She shared that many of her clients are worried about being killed in school. She thinks this is why many kids are having a hard time going to school. "There is a pervasive sense of hopelessness in many of the children I work with—it is so sad." She added, "One of my adolescent boys told me he feels like he is in prison during lockdown drills."

Teachers are only human, and they face great challenges physically and mentally in the arena of school safety. It is unfair to place the entire burden of saving lives on teachers; school administrations need to provide supportive education for both the actual drills and dealing with the emotional well-being of their students.

For all of us, there is much work to be done. Obviously, it's important that you stay informed about what is happening at your child's school. If their school currently does not have a policy of letting parents know that a lockdown drill took place during the day, speak with your administrators and request it. Encourage other parents to speak up as well.

CHAPTER 4

Virtual Violence: Is It Really Bad?

Children who consume too much violent imagery are put at risk, sometimes even copying acts of violence experienced during game play. In fact, most scientific studies link exposure to violent video games and aggression in children.[1,2]

In the summer of 2018, you may have heard about a disturbing new video game called *Active Shooter*. It is an interactive school shooting simulation in which you can pick sides—either as a member of the SWAT team or the person trying to kill people at a school or elsewhere. Marketing for the game, which was developed by Revived Games and published by a Russian company called Acid, proclaimed, "Pick your role, gear up and fight or destroy! Your objective would be either to neutralize the target (active shooter) or be the target himself. Slaughter as many civilians as possible, as well as forces that are against you! The choice is yours!" Acid had planned to sell the game for between five and ten dollars on the Steam platform.

The advertising for the game also carried the advice, "Please do not take any of this seriously. This is only meant to be the simulation and nothing else. If you feel like hurting someone or people around you, please seek help from local psychiatrists or dial 911 (or applicable)."

Responsible of them, right?

Thousands of people signed a petition against release of the game,

1 "Violent Video Games Make Children More Violent," Centre for Educational Neuroscience, University College London, http://www.educationalneuroscience.org.uk/resources/neuromyth-or-neurofact/violent-video-games-make-children-more-violent/.

2 Sylvie Mrug, Anjana Madan, Edwin W. Cook III, et al,"Emotional and Physiological Desensitization to Real-Life and Movie Violence," National Institutes of Health, 2014, https://www.ncbi.nlm.nih.gov/pmc/articles/PMC4393354/.

ultimately putting pressure on Acid. Fortunately, *Active Shooter* was pulled from distribution just days before it was supposed to hit the market due to public outcry, though the company says that it still may be released someday.[3]

This is what we and our children are up against. The American Psychological Association reports that more than 90 percent of children in the United States play video games. Among kids between the ages of 12 and 17, the number rises to 97 percent. More importantly, at least 85 percent of video games on the market contain some form of violence.[4]

I am certain you know if your kids are playing games that contain inappropriate images and violent activities. Exposure to extreme and excessive violence is detrimental to their physical and emotional well-being.

What Is "Virtual Violence"?

The American Academy of Pediatrics uses the term "virtual violence" to discuss all forms of violence that are not experienced physically. This encompasses screen-based violence that is more realistic than ever before. Virtual violence includes first-person shooter games and other realistic video games and applications.[5]

Kids develop many of the necessary skills they need in order to have a productive and happy life during childhood. In my experience, being consumed with computer games and/or social media limits the developing brain's creativity, self-confidence, resilience, compassion, empathy, and enjoyment of physical activity, to list just a few issues. This helps to create the perfect storm for anxiety, a depressed mood, Vitamin D deficiency, a sense of having no purpose, lack of resiliance, and even suicidal tendencies.

---

[3] "Valve—Do not Launch Active Shooter—A School Shooter Video Game," Change.org petition, https://www.change.org/p/valve-corporation-do-not-launch-active-shooter-a-school-shooter-video-game.

[4] "Resolution on Violent Video Games," American Psychological Association, 2015, https://www.apa.org/about/policy/violent-video-games.aspx.

[5] Dimitri Christakis, "Virtual Violence: Council on Communications and Media," Pediatrics, October 1, 2016, http://pediatrics.aappublications.org/content/early/2016/07/14/peds.2016-1298.

In addition, when children and teens play violent video games, they intellectually understand that it is not real violence and killing, but their nervous systems don't know the difference. Their bodies respond as if they were in a real, dangerous situation. They are stressing the nervous system. This is one of the greatest risks of children spending endless hours playing, or watching other people play, violent video games.

Here's what happens biologically: The *amygdala*, an almond shaped structure deep in the brain's emotional center, known as the limbic system, looks for incoming signals that may be predictors of stress. If any stress is picked up, the amygdala sends alert messages to the body including a *fight or flight* reaction. The *hypothalamus*, a tiny region at the base of the brain, sets off an alarm system in the body. Through a combination of nerve and hormonal signals, this system prompts the adrenal glands to release a surge of hormones, including adrenaline and cortisol.[6]

Adrenaline increases heart rate, elevates blood pressure, and boosts energy supplies. *Cortisol*, the primary stress hormone, enhances the brain's use of glucose and increases sugars in the bloodstream and the availability of substances that repair tissues. It alters immune system responses and suppresses the digestive system, the reproductive system, and growth processes.

After so much exposure to violence, even if it is in games or movies, it becomes hard for the brain and the body to decipher when a crisis has passed. The real danger is if the "fight or flight" response is being made impotent by consistently playing violent games. This means that the child may know that the "threat" is over, but his or her brain hasn't signaled the body that it is safe to calm down. This can lead to a child feeling mentally exhausted by so much exposure to violence that if a true dangerous situation does occur, he or she may not be able to respond in the safest way.

There is a good chance that if you are letting your children spend countless hours playing or watching violence, you are enabling them to

---

[6] "Chronic Stress Puts Your Health at Risk," Mayo Clinic, https://www.mayoclinic.org/healthy-lifestyle/stress-management/in-depth/stress/art-20046037.

feel stressed out, tired, irritable, angry, and for some, emotionally and physically unwell.

The American Psychological Association passed a resolution in 2015 declaring that "scientific research has demonstrated an association between violent video game use and both increases in aggressive behavior, aggressive affect, aggressive cognitions and decreases in behaviors that include empathy, and moral engagement," among other findings. The American Academy of Pediatrics continues to be concerned about children's exposure to virtual violence and the effect it has on their overall health and well-being.

Pam, a fellow psychotherapist who lives near Parkland, Florida, tells parents that once their child is subjected to violent or oversexualized images, those can't be erased from his or her mind. A metaphor for this may be squeezing a toothpaste tube: Once the toothpaste is out, you can't get it back in.

I had the privilege to speak with Pam on several occasions during the months after the shooting in Parkland. She told me that during that horrible day, students pulled out their phones and recorded teachers and students being shot and killed. Within thirty minutes of the shootings, her daughter saw a video of a Marjory Stoneman Douglas High School student dying in real time. As most of us know, those videos went viral. She added, "Once our children are exposed to violence, there is no going back." She continued to state that she blames social media for helping to glamorize violence.

Joy, a mom of a middle school age daughter, told me a frightening story. Her daughter told her that she was friends with a girl who she met through a mutual friend in one of their Snapchat groups. Although she had spent a lot of time texting with her and even FaceTiming, she confided to her mom that lately this girl was "freaking" her out. After much convincing, Joy's daughter confessed that her new friend talked about how she engaged in self-harming behaviors such as cutting, and even mentioned suicide. Joy was unable to determine the real identity of this girl. She couldn't even figure out what town or state she lived in. Nobody in the daughter's Snapchat group knew who she was, or even how she joined. Joy insisted that her daughter unfollow her. The only thing Joy could do was to set up a better system of reviewing her daughter's social media friends.

Joy encouraged me to share this story with parents as a heads-up to what is going on in the worlds of many children. She added that she regularly reviews with her daughter who she has accepted as friends and followers.

Let's imagine the impact on all of the kids who accepted this guy's request. Those who already were traumatized are re-traumatized. The image of this boy holding a gun affects the brain, which signals their body, and the child may be left feeling anxious, scared, depressed, and terribly upset.

A Huge Parenting Dilemma

All of this technology has created a huge parenting dilemma: It seems that we have surrendered our parenting power to technological devices, which is a real factor in the violence we are seeing all too often in schools today.

Many parents seem overwhelmed and even defensive when I point out the correlation between playing violent video games and violent behavior. Their reaction leads me to wonder if they feel powerless to control their kids' addiction to playing the games. One parent told me that they are concerned about the amount of time their eighth-grade son plays *Fortnite*, but "everyone plays it" and they don't want him to be left out of the social scene.

Another mom seemed relieved that her socially anxious ninth-grade son finally had friends. Every day after school, he came home and got right on his computer. "He puts his fancy headphones on and I don't really know who he is playing with. He tells me he is playing with his friends." She (and you) should stop and consider this:

+ Is he playing with friends from his school?

- Have you ever met any of these kids?

- Are they actually other kids, or adults pretending to be kids?

- How much money is he spending on video games? On tokens?

- Is he using his own money or does he have your credit card number?

- Do you check how much money he is spending per week, per month?

These are all extremely important questions to ask any child who is playing video games. All over the world there are many unsavory characters that pose as other teens. You need to monitor how much time your child is spending, and with whom.

An eleven-year-old girl told me she has a problem with cursing too much. When I asked where she learned such offensive words, she says, "I have a seventeen-year-old brother who is addicted to *Fortnite*. I hear him saying horrible words to his friends. He thinks we can't hear him just because he has his headphones on. I can hear him cursing throughout the house."

I am worried for these kids. I am worried for the anxious child who struggles to make friends and who spends endless hours playing video games.

A few years ago, while I was speaking to a group of parents, a soft-spoken woman raised her hand and asked what she could do about her teenage son's obsession with video games. He barely slept or ate and often refused to go to school complaining that he was too tired from staying up all night gaming, mom assumed. She said that she brought him his food on a tray. She would knock on his door to let him know that there was food outside. He then would shout at her to go away. Eventually, he would take the tray inside and slam the door shut.

Another woman in the audience joined in; she had a similar situation with her son. She and her husband decided to cut off their Wi-Fi, which stopped her son from connecting to the games. She added that this was a disaster. He got violent, pushed her down, and threw furniture. It got so bad that she had to call the police.

The police informed her son that if they were called again, he would be arrested for domestic violence. The woman said that the police officer suggested she seek professional help for her son since he was displaying addictive behavior.

I looked at these scared moms and felt their anguish. They didn't realize that when they bought their children an Xbox or the latest game that they were handing them a drug—one that is very addictive for some kids. (I can almost guarantee that if your child was addicted to a drug you would not remain quiet. So don't remain quiet now.)

After I finished speaking at the program, I provided the parents with community resources available to help children who are addicted to technology. A growing number of rehabilitation centers opening throughout the country are specifically designed to help people with screen addictions. I discuss these resources in Chapter 8, "Benefiting from Community."

A Sense of Helplessness

A consistent theme I hear is that many parents feel helpless in the task of enforcing rules and limits with their children, and helpless against the societal tide.

"If I don't permit my son to play video games, in essence it will be like he is committing social suicide."

"All the kids are playing it—so how bad could it be?"

A mother told me that her son was struggling with feelings of anxiety that often made it really challenging for him to separate from her. He also was having difficulty finding friends with whom he felt comfortable. In an effort to help her son to try and fit in with his peers, she gave him the latest video game technology. (He was only eight years old.)

One day her son came home from school crying hysterically and demanding that they move. One of the boys with whom he was playing video games decided to have a few laughs by digitally pasting her son's face on an anonymous boy's body. The end result looked like a photo of her son sitting on the toilet. In no time, this photo made the rounds of the virtual world.

The mom explained that she felt guilty that she couldn't protect him from the outside world, and it happened in her own house.

I am certain that scenarios like this play out every day throughout the world. It is so commonplace that I wonder how many kids share their stories with their parents. How many are left feeling victimized and helpless? How many children are "alone" in dealing with these complicated and often traumatizing situations, and how will it affect their ability to deal with the much more serious issues besieging today's schools?

What is *Fortnite, Battle Royale?*

The hottest video game at the time of this writing is *Fortnite*, marketed by privately held Epic Games, Inc. Ask any boy and some girls, eight years old or older, what game they are playing these days and the answer will be *Fortnite*. Most will add, "Don't worry, it isn't violent."

I decided to check out *Fortnite*. I went to a few parenting websites that I trust to see how they describe this video game. My favorite site is Common Sense Media,[7] and here's what they have to say about this product:

> *Fortnite* is a video game for PlayStation 4, Xbox One, Windows, Mac, and mobile that takes elements from sandbox-building games and adds the fast-paced action of a third-person shooter. There are two modes to the game: a solo version called *Save the World* and the hugely popular multiplayer version called *Battle Royale*. If your kids are playing *Fortnite*, they're probably playing *Battle Royale*, the free-

---

[7] https://www.commonsensemedia.org

to-play multiplayer offshoot of the game. In this version, up to 100 people can participate together in a match.[8]

In short, it's a mass online brawl where players leap out of a plane onto a small island and then fight each other until only one has survived. Apparently, hidden around the islands are weapons including crossbows, rifles, and grenade launchers. Players must arm themselves while exploring the landscape and buildings to collect resources that allow them to build structures where they can hide or defend themselves. As the match progresses, the playable area of land is continually reduced forcing players closer and closer together. The last survivor is the winner.[9]

According to Nick Paumgarten's May 21, 2018 article in the *New Yorker* magazine, *Fortnite* has become the most viewed game on YouTube. By March 2018, there had been almost three billion views of the millions of sessions that players had uploaded.[10] As of July 2018, *Fortnite* celebrated its one-year anniversary by announcing it has 125 million players and over $1 billion in revenue.[11]

Parents should assume that both boys and girls are playing video games on their phones as well as other devices. According to The Statistia Portal, women accounted for nearly 45 percent of American gamers in 2018, a slight increase over the previous year.[12]

If your child is not playing *Fortnite*, then he or she may be playing *Call of Duty* or a similar video game, whether on a console, a phone, or on a computer. It is also a big trend for kids to spend hours upon hours watching YouTube videos of kids and adults they don't know playing video games.

---

[8] Frannie Occiferri, "Parents' Ultimate Guide to Fortnite," Common Sense Media, October 15, 2018, https://www.commonsensemedia.org/blog/parents-ultimate-guide-to-fortnite.

[9] Keith Stuart, "Fortnite: A Parents' Guide to the Most Popular Video Game in Schools," *The Guardian*, March 7, 2018, https://www.theguardian.com/games/2018/mar/07/fortnite-battle-royale-parents-guide-video-game-multiplayer-shooter.

[10] Nick Paumgarten, "How Fortnite Captured Teens' Hearts and Minds," *The New Yorker*, May 21, 2018.

[11] Huddleston Jr., Tom, "Fortnite' Just Hit its One-Year Anniversary—How the Billion-Dollar Game Is Celebrating its Birthday," CNBC, July 24, 2018, https://www.cnbc.com/2018/07/24/fortnite-one-year-anniversary-how-billion-dollar-game-is-celebrating.html.

[12] "Distribution of Computer and Video Gamers in the United States from 2006 to 2018, by Gender," Statista, The Statistics Portal, http://www.statista.com/statistics/195754/number-of-us-gamers-per-platform.

In a blog for *Thrillist Entertainment,* Joshua Khan and Leanne Butkovic stated that video games "are four times more expensive than movies, three times the commitment of a TV show, and usually require intense concentration to make it past the character selection phase (hard look at you, *Monster Hunter: World*). But all of that's exactly why they can be so rewarding when you find one that matches your taste."[13]

YouTube

If you have kids, YouTube may be your in-house babysitter, your kid's companion, and possibly his or her best friend. If you are not that familiar with YouTube, I highly suggest you start learning about it. There are hundreds of YouTube channels, YouTube stars, YouTube games, and much more.

Dr. Deborah Heitner, author of *Screenwise: Helping Kids Thrive (and Survive) in Their Digital World,* and of the article, "What Kids are Really Watching on YouTube (and How Parents Can Deal with It)," asks a great question:

"What are you kids watching on YouTube anyway?" she writes. "Your kid has been staring at his tablet for hours. When you ask what he's watching, he answers 'YouTube.' When he first logged on, you saw him watching another kid unwrapping some brand-new toys. Thirty minutes later, you hear your child laughing hysterically. You wonder, 'What is he watching now? Is that toy video really that hilarious?'" She urges parents to be mindful of what their children are watching, and suggests how to engage them in talking about what they are seeing.[14]

Dr. Heitner confirms that many parents already are concerned with what their kids are watching, and from my experience, they should be. YouTube Kids has been criticized for inappropriate content, including pornography, inappropriate language, and disturbing material.

---

[13] Joshua Khan and Leanne Butkovic, "The Best Video Games of 2018 (So Far)," Thrilllist, https://www.thrillist.com/entertainment/nation/best-video-games-2018.

[14] Devorah Heitner, "What Kids are Really Watching on YouTube (and How Parents Can Deal With It)," Raising Digital Natives, http://www.raisingdigitalnatives.com/youtube-parenting.

Know what your child is watching. Here are a few of the popular YouTube Kids channels according to Statista[15].

+ ChuChu TV Nursery Rhymes and Kids Songs

+ ToyPudding TV

+ Ryan ToysReview

+ FunToys Collector Disney Toys Review

Here are some of the channels you should view before your kids do. These carry content that can be violent, drug-related, and sexual:

+ AngryJoeShow

+ SuperMarioLogan—it is full of yelling, inappropriate language

+ Angry Video Game Nerd—nasty language from an angry guy

There are many more inappropriate videos. Simply do a Google search and watch some. I was horrified by the nasty voices as well as the language.

Viewing these videos can confuse children. The child thinks, "I am used to one thing, this video shows another; this doesn't make sense," and experiences anxiety. In Zoe Bernard's recent article for *Business Insider*,[16] she claimed that YouTube is providing kids with thousands of disturbing, violent, and inappropriate videos, and is reportedly doing nothing about it.

James Bridle, in an article posted for the online magazine *Medium*, writes that YouTube broadcasters have developed a huge number of tactics to draw parents' and children's attention to their videos and the advertising revenues that accompany them. He states, "someone or

15 "Most Popular Children-Themed YouTube Channels as of September 2018," Statistica, September 2018. http://www.statista.com/statistics/785626/most-popular-youtube-children-channels-ranked-by-subscribers.

16 Zoe Bernard, "YouTube Is Reportedly Pointing Kids to Thousands of Disturbing, Violent, and Inappropriate Videos," *Business Insider*, November 8, 2017, https://www.businessinsider.com/youtube-has-thousands-of-disturbing-videos-targeted-at-kids-report-2017-11.

something or some combination of people and things is using YouTube to systematically frighten, traumatize, and abuse children, automatically and at scale, and it forces me to question my own beliefs about the internet, at every level."[17]

It is up to you to decide what role YouTube will play in your child's life.

What Can a Parent Do?

Many parents express frustration and a sense of helplessness about the popularity of games like *Fortnite* and *Call of Duty*, as well as violent games available on YouTube and elsewhere.

There are parents who permit their kids to play violent video games, but are concerned about the amount of time spent on them. There are others who in principle are against their kids playing violent video games, but feel that it would be unfair and social suicide if they did not let their kids play them.

After speaking with parents from various cities and small towns throughout the country, I found that there is an enormous disconnect between the fact that we are experiencing a rise in school shootings, and kids' addiction, preoccupation, and dependence on their technological devices. The majority of parents I spoke with resist monitoring both the content of the violent games, shows, and movies their kids are viewing, as well as the various sites where they hang out.

If you give your kid devices, you need to be prepared to monitor them.

What was this resistance about monitoring and setting limits on kids really about? Why are so many parents reluctant to monitor their kids' gaming activity level?

---

[17] James Bridle, "Something Is Wrong on the Internet," *Medium*, November 6, 2017, https://medium.com/@jamesbridle/something-is-wrong-on-the-internet-c39c471271d2.

Often, parents are fearful that if they set limits and controls on technology usage, their children will freak out. "Nancy, you won't believe how he behaves when I turn off the game. He starts screaming, throwing things around the room; once he even threw himself against the wall. He never acted this way when he was three or four years old, but now he is thirteen. I don't know what to do."

I have heard many versions of this story from distressed parents over and over again. Parents report that when they take away their children's tablets or attempt to stop them from playing video games, they get violent. If your child becomes violent on more than the rare occasion, you have a problem.

Is Your Child Addicted to Screen Time? A Short Quiz

Take a minute to answer these questions:
- Does your child walk around with his head down staring at his device while brushing his teeth or walking to school?
- Does your child forget to do some of her personal hygiene tasks?
- Does your child rush home from school to start playing video games?
- Does your child throw a tantrum that would make a three-year-old look quiet?
- Do you feel like your life is being controlled by your child's addiction to gaming?
- Has your child lost interest in activities that used to bring him or her joy?
- Is your child's gaming habit interfering with academic success?
- Do you spend less time with your child?

If you answered yes to some of these questions, please

pay attention carefully. It is not too late to take charge of this situation. Don't throw your hands up waiting for this "phase" to pass. It may pass, or it may not.

All of this addiction to electronic devices is literally altering the brain. A study, "Microstructure Abnormalities in Adolescents with Internet Addiction Disorder (IAD)" by Kai Yuan, suggests that long-term internet addiction results in brain structural alterations, which probably contributes to chronic dysfunction in subjects with IAD.[18]

In the article, "Gray Matters: Too Much Screen Time Damages the Brain," Dr. Victoria L. Dunckley reports areas affected include the frontal lobe, which governs executive functions, planning, prioritizing, organizing, and impulse control. She claims research indicates that screen time contributes to socially unacceptable impulses, and suppresses the capacity to develop empathy and compassion. She also states there is research indicating that damage to the *insula*, a region of the brain deep in the cerebral cortex, is the possible connection to violent behavior.[19]

In 2007, Microsoft founder Bill Gates implemented a cap on screen time when his daughter started developing an unhealthy attachment to a video game. He also didn't let his kids get cell phones until they turned fourteen. (Today, the average age when a child gets their first phone is ten.) Apple founder Steve Jobs revealed in a 2011 *New York Times* interview that he prohibited his kids from using the newly-released iPad. "We limit how much technology our kids use at home," Jobs told reporter Nick Bilton.[20]

---

[18] Kai Yuan, Wei Qin, Guihong Wang, et al, "Microstructure Abnormalities in Adolescents with Internet Addiction Disorder," Plos, June 3, 2011, https://journals.plos.org/plosone/article?id=10.1371/journal.pone.0020708.

[19] Victoria Dunckley, "Gray Matters: Too Much Screen Time Damages the Brain," *Psychology Today*, February 27, 2014, https://www.psychologytoday.com/us/blog/mental-wealth/201402/gray-matters-too-much-screen-time-damages-the-brain.

[20] Chris Weller, "Bill Gates and Steve Jobs Raised Their Kids Tech-Free,—and It Should've Been a Red Flag," *Business Insider*, https://www.independent.co.uk/life-style/gadgets-and-tech/bill-gates-and-steve-jobs-raised-their-kids-techfree-and-it-shouldve-been-a-red-flag-a8017136.html.

Despite those high-visibility statements on the importance of restricting screen time for kids, usage has increased exponentially. As I write this book, numerous times a day I look out my office window and see children and adults walking with their heads down, staring at their devices. Rarely do I have a therapy session with a client that is not interrupted by a beep, ding, or melody playing from their phone or electronic watch.

Risky Social Media Apps

Let's talk about the virtual playground your kids are hanging out in these days.

Keeping up on the latest places your kids are hanging out on social media, whether it is Snapchat, Instagram, Tinder, or Amino, can be a daunting task. There is a good chance that your child is spending a lot of time on many apps, and is probably hiding a few from you. Keep in mind that most apps have inherent risks. Messages and pictures on these apps are easily deleted after being received or sent. Plus, it's very common for kids to create fake accounts on Instagram, Pinterest, and Tumblr, not only to hide them from you, but to connect with people with whom you would have real issues.

I met with a teen who was in the process of exploring her sexuality. She spent a lot of time creating fake accounts as she connected with other people, hoping no one would be able to track them back to her. These apps are addictive and seductive, their sites are flooded with images of perfect bodies, flawless skin, and often violent images.

Let's be honest, many of this apps are designed to appeal to the developing teenage mind, preying on their need for independence, their feelings of stress, loneliness, and wanting to feel they belong.

What Are the Most Dangerous Apps?

There also are scores of mobile phone, iPad, and Kindle apps that can be harmful to your kids' well-being.

EducateEmpowerKids.org is a nonprofit that provides resources for parents and educators to encourage deep connection with their kids through media education, meaningful family communication, and intentional parenting. They believe this must be done by teaching digital citizenship, media literacy, and healthy sexuality education—including education about the dangers of online pornography. They offer online resources and community workshops across the country to improve the digital lives of kids.

On their site I found an extremely helpful lists of apps that parents need to know about.

 **Instagram:** Owned by Facebook, this is an extremely popular social media app for sharing personal photos and videos. *Finstagram* is a secondary, fake Instagram account that kids create in order to keep their interactions away from your prying eyes. Kids often share this with a smaller circle of followers, often posting photos or videos that are funny or embarrassing, sexy, etc.

A *finsta* account can gives you a window into your child's inner world. These accounts usually display unfiltered and unedited versions of its users. Kids share their most private struggles, their dreams, their complaints about you, and everything else that goes through their mind. Think of it as similar to our generation's use of a diary.

While your child's real Instagram account, or *rinsta*, may be open to the public, a finsta is private and more selective. They often use a fake, clever username and allow themselves to be more "real" on this account. Some teens even give their friends their passwords, which can backfire if they get into a disagreement about something.

A post may go like this: "Did that really cute boy you have a crush on look at you at lunch? (Psst, I read it on your private Finstagram with the fake account I created to spy on you.) Do you think he liked your new yoga pants?"

If you want to know if your child has a Finstagram—ask. That is always the best place to start.

Instagram has created a way for people to switch back and forth between accounts without logging out of one and logging into another. Here is how to do it: Look at the app on their phone. Click on their profile icon and then look next to their username at the top. If there is an arrow next to it, click on it. If there are other accounts, they will show up.

Tinder: Tinder is a dating app where users create a short description about themselves, upload a photo, and have access to other people's photos and information. Users engage on the app by "swiping right" to those who they wish to get to know, and "swiping left" to those they are not interested in. Users receive a notification when they receive a "match," meaning that the person they swiped right on also swiped right to their photo.[21] They claim to be the largest, hottest community of singles in the world. "We are called the world's hottest app for a reason…we spark more 26 million matches per day," states Tinder's description in the Apple app store.[22]

Recently, a high school senior told me that she is on Tinder. "Everyone makes a Tinder account in their freshmen year of high school," she said.

Kik: Kik is a free messaging app with over 300 million users and stands out from other mobile messaging apps because its accounts are based on usernames without the need for a phone or phone number.[23] You log in and can send texts, selfies, and emojis to your friends. It is often

---

[21] Amy Morin, "What every Parent Needs to Know about Tinder," verywellfamily, November 19, 2017, https://www.verywellfamily.com/what-every-parent-needs-to-know-about-tinder-2609052.

[22] Tinder Description, Apple App Store.

[23] "What Every Parent Needs to Know About Kik," TeenSafe, November 30, 2015, https://www.teensafe.com/blog/everything-a-parent-needs-to-know-about-kik.

referred to as a "chat app." Kik provides free, easy, and instant connections to other users, and also allows anonymous people to contact children. Thus, parents have no way of knowing who is contacting their kids, and no way to keep them safe. It's not uncommon for users to receive nude or violent photos.[24]

Kik's scariest components include Porn Bots, automated programs that disguise themselves as suggestive, personalized messages to trick users into clicking on porn sites; and Chat Now, which allows anonymous users to contact your child.[25]

Amino: This app allows viewers to participate in online communities focused on similar interests. Is your kid into Star Wars, Minecraft, watching porn stars, or learning how to vape? The app includes features for chatting, messaging, picture sharing and more—all with strangers.

Live.ly: This is a live streaming app. Users create content and broadcast live to viewers that do not need to register any personal information or provide age verification. Your child has no idea who is able to access his or her "live stream," and has access to others' live streams that often contain nudity and offensive language and behavior.

Musical.ly: This sister site to Live.ly is super-popular with kids in elementary and middle school. It is promoted as a fun app for "kids" to lip synch and create their own music videos to share. There is no age verification. Kids just need a phone number,

---

[24] "Kik Messenger: Why This App Is Trouble for Teens," *SmartSocial*, February 29, 2016, https://smartsocial.com/kik-messenger-app-trouble-teens.

[25] "Everything a Parent Needs to Know About Kik," *SmartSocial*, November 30, 2015, https://www.teensafe.com/blog/everything-a-parent-needs-to-know-about-kik/.

an account with Facebook or Instagram, or an email (any of which are not hard to fake) to sign up. Everyone now has easy access to your child's profile. I have heard that there is a lot of inappropriate media, pornography, and bullying on Musical.ly—and not always kid-to-kid, but adults bullying kids, as well.

Omegle: This app claims to offer a great way to meet new friends. "When you use Omegle, we pick someone else at random and let you talk one-on-one." In bold letters its description states "Video is monitored. Keep it clean!" It also advises that predators have been known to use Omegle, "…so please be careful". In smaller print it says not to use Omegle if you are under thirteen years old, and if you are under eighteen years old, get your parents' permission."[26] It is an online forum in which strangers are paired supposedly based on similar interests and can chat via messages and video. The typical chat starts with "ASL": Age? Sex? Location? A teen I spoke with told me, "Don't even open Omegle, you won't approve of it."

Yubo (formerly called Yellow)—Make New Friends: This is a free app allowing users to connect (flirt) with others in their local area, similar to Tinder. There is no age verification to use the app, and it links up with Snapchat and Instagram, allowing strangers complete access to profile information and pictures.[27]

Hot or Not: This is a comparison and rating app. People send in photos of themselves to be rated by others, and have the opportunity to view the "hottest" users in their area and connect with them. I really hate this one.

---

[26] Omegle Description, https://www.omegle.com.

[27] Yubo Description, https://itunes.apple.com/us/app/yubo-make-new-friends/id1038653883?mt=8.

Ask.fm: Currently ASKfm is the biggest Q&A discussion platform in the world, claiming they have more than 215 million registered members in 168 countries who can easily communicate and gain experience by corresponding with others from within their peer group without having to worry about social awkwardness or shyness. This site has been linked to some of the worst cases of cyberbullying. There is no way to know who is following you or who posted the question. Additionally:

+ Users can ask questions anonymously in the app. Some users have asked how to kill or cut themselves, and so forth, and then others provide answers on how to do it.

+ Sharing content is easy, since Ask.fm is friendly with Facebook and Twitter. It's just one click between sharing on a social media platform where things are *not* anonymous, to an environment that is.

+ Some claim that Ask.fm is the best formatted social media platform to provide help answers to kids.

+ This is not an app that is popular with parents but is gaining traction with children and teens because they want their own forum to engage with their peers.

Vora: According to the Apple Store review site, the name, "Vora" refers to voraciously devouring a big meal after fasting.[28] This is a dieting app that allows users to track their fasting activity. It has become very popular with kids who are dealing with eating disorders. The app has a so-  cial media feature that connects the user with other fasters by creating profiles. Users connect with one another on a Facebook user page. They can then encourage each other to extend their fasts. I am not a big fan of this one!

---

[28] https://blog.securly.com/2018/06/19/popular-teen-apps-parents-need-to-know-part-2/

 **Hiding Apps:** These apps allow users to hide messages, pictures, and other content. Private Photo Calculator, Gallery Lock Lite, Best Secret Folder, and Keep Safe are a few. They show up as an innocuous icon, such as calculator or clock when someone else logs into the phone. There are many similar apps in this category. Kids are famous for hiding information from their parents and their friends on some of these apps.

Tips for Managing Apps on Your Child's Phone

- Remind your child to never share their home address or phone number with anyone they don't personally know.

- Don't respond to people they do not know—even if they say they are a friend of so-and-so. It is easy to look at your child's account and see who their "friends" are.

- Empower them to BLOCK any users they don't know, that make them feel uncomfortable, or ones they just don't want to connect with.

- Set up scheduled and unscheduled time to sit down with your child and go over what's on their phone. Monitoring is key to helping your child develop and maintain healthy virtual experiences.

Becky's Story

Over the years, I have heard many hair-raising stories of how young people utilize the internet to learn disturbing and destructive things. Take Becky, who became fascinated with hanging out in some dark and creepy sites as well as chat rooms. She learned how to *cut*—the act of using a sharp item such as a razor or a piece of broken glass to cut on one's own arm, leg, or stomach—for the goal of inflicting pain. There are sites that provide guides and videos on how to do it and there are places to go to meet other "cutters."

Eventually, Becky got bored with cutting and moved on to meetup sites. By the time I met her, she had spent time on sex sites where older men met young girls, sites where men like overweight girls, etc.

There is no doubt that before the age of the internet, teens could find trouble if they went looking for it. The difference today is that they can find it at the tap of the finger—and the community of sketchy and disturbing predators now extends well beyond your local neighborhood or town to cover the world.

A 3D Gun

You may have heard the news about 3D printers. 3D printers are machines often priced in the $100 to $300 range with which you can create a three-dimensional object from a digital file that can be obtained from the internet. These machines actually can manufacture guns! The common term for a 3D-printed firearm is "ghost gun," which refers to the fact that these firearms are printed without serial numbers and are virtually untraceable by the government.[29]

Susan Jaffe Prober, head of information services at the Millburn, New Jersey, free public library, told me that a man in his twenties wanted to use the library's recently obtained 3D printer to create part of an AR-15 rifle. When the librarian on duty at the time received the request, she quickly told the man that it was against the library's policy to print guns. "The librarian showed him the policy. The man became frustrated with the response, and said he would go to another library," she told me. "The librarian stayed calm during the interaction but after he left she was shaken."

Prober shared that the library board had the good sense in 2015 when it first placed an order for the 3D printer to develop a policy that

---

[29] "2018 3D Printed Gun Report—All You Need to Know," All3DP, https://all3dp.com/3d-printed-gun-firearm-weapon-parts/

prohibited "the printing of objects that are unsafe, harmful, dangerous, or pose immediate threat to the safety and well-being of others." She also added that it appeared that that the man was not a regular visitor of the library.

On August 27, 2018, *The New York Times* reported that Cory Wilson, a "self-described crypto-anarchist," who tried for years to post blueprints for 3D printed guns online had to keep waiting, thanks to a judge who upheld a restraining order, aligning with attorneys general from nineteen states and Washington, D.C., who contend that 3D-printed guns constitute a threat to national safety.[30]

However, during my research on 3D guns, it took me less than one minute to end up on a site that would allow me to start downloading a template for free. Scary stuff. Talk to your kids about 3D guns, and what to do if someone is talking about making one. Share your feelings about the risks of owning an unlicensed gun.

Some Tips to Stay on Top of the Situation

There's no doubt that virtual violence—whether through unhealthy, socially destructive apps or violent video games—is contributing to the rising phenomenon of angry, aggressive, socially uncomfortable children and, by extension, rise of violence in our schools. Here are a few things you can do to better regulate your kids' participation in these dangerous activities.

+ Educate yourself. At least once a month, do a quick online search for "new social media apps." Set up a policy that your children have to ask permission to download a new app. Check out the app before you allow them to download it. Don't give yourself permission for excuses, no matter how busy, how stressed out you are, or how bad you are with technology. You need to educate yourself and pay attention.

---

[30] Tiffany Hsu, "3-D Printed Gun Plans Must Stay Off Internet for Now, Judge Rules," *The New York Times*, August 27, 2018, https://www.nytimes.com/2018/08/27/business/3-d-printed-gun-cody-wilson.html.

+ Discuss the apps or sites you find with your kids, ask them what they know, and keep the lines of communication open.

+ Talk to your kids about the changes that happen to their brains when they consume too much screen time, particularly violent images.

+ Say "No" to certain games that you do not want in your home.

+ Set time limits.

+ Give your kids constructive feedback on their behavior when they spend too much time consuming violent stimuli.

+ Conduct weekly meetings with your family focusing on what apps your kids are using, how much time they are spending, and what they are missing out on because they are spending so much time on their devices.

+ Educate your children on the dangers of "oversharing" online. Teach them that every comment, every picture, every search, is documented online and remains there forever.

+ Create a family contract governing the use of games, social media, and other internet-based activities. Know everyone's passwords. (That's non-negotiable.) Set appropriate parental controls, age restrictions for downloading apps, and time restrictions.

+ Again, check your kids' devices frequently and thoroughly. Connect to all of the apps from your child's device. View the child's activity, messages, contacts, etc.

+ Use community resources. Many local communities have workshops on how to keep your child safe on the internet. Attend a workshop with your child/teen. View a safety video online together.

Pay Attention and Take Action

It is deeply concerning that too many children spend the majority of their leisure time playing or watching others play violent video games. Children are growing up spending an inordinate amount of their waking lives literally in a fantasy, creating make-believe characters who fight, kill, and get killed in this make-believe place. All this continues to trigger their brains into a fight or flight response, which not only stresses out their nervous system, but may be desensitizing them to violence. I worry if a child who has spent much time in this make-believe violent world would actually know what to do if a real-life trauma or school shooting happened. Then they would not be a created character, but just themselves—stripped of their armor of weapons and magic powers.

Just like most things in life, "everything in moderation" applies to video games, especially those with violent content. It is crucial to monitor age-appropriateness as well as the amount of time your child is devoting to his or her "addiction."

I sat down on the couch, sandwiching myself between my two adorable grandnieces, Olivia, age three, and Julia, age four, as they stared at the big screen before us. The two girls held onto my arms for dear life as they watched a movie that was not age-appropriate. I sat there for maybe three minutes before I was unable to keep my mouth shut. "This is so scary," I said. "Let's go outside and play." I couldn't get either one of the girls to move. "Doesn't this make you feel yucky inside?" I asked.

Julia answered, "I have lots of bad dreams."

Olivia nodded her head yes.

I got up to retrieve my niece. My motto of only giving advice to my clients went out the window as I expressed my concern for the girls watching such scary things. She immediately walked into the family room and said, "Come on girls, we are going outside, no more movie." The girls bounced up and followed us outside leaving the older sister, age six, clearly very upset that I ruined her fun.

There is no gain, no benefit for children, especially young children, to be consumers of violent content. Parents, please pay attention to what your kids are watching, what they are playing, and what they are viewing on their electronics! The bottom line is that it is not making them happier.

CHAPTER 5

Talking to Your Kids About Violence

There are many things that keep parents up at night: financial concerns, medical issues, learning challenges, and social issues. Those concerns often take second place to worrying about what has previously been a totally unthinkable question, "Will my child be killed at school?"

The most important tool you have in this climate of fear is yourself. The best investment you can make, better than the right soccer coach or math tutor, is devoting time and energy to helping your child learn to deal with life's challenges. I have found that the kids who best demonstrate resilience, empathy, and motivation are those whose parents spend significant quality time with them, and understand the most comforting way to talk with them about today's school violence issues.

I frequently suggest to parents that they use humor as part of their parenting tool kit. This is always sure to stir up some reactions. Some parents get defensive declaring, "I *am* funny, my kids think I am funny." Others state, "Parenting is serious business. Children need to know that they have responsibilities and must do them."

I don't disagree. But I do believe that parenting is all about the relationship that you build with your child. Humor gives us the opportunity to laugh at ourselves and not to sound as if we are being judgmental or critical, a drill sergeant, or just trying too hard to be "cool."

The threat of potential school violence is as scary as it gets. How are you going to arm yourself with knowledge, compassion, and wit to get an "A" on this job?

Helpful Tools When Speaking to Your Child

You can best help your children feel comfortable and secure by implementing some basic guidelines in your conversations with them. Put down your phone and look your child in the eyes. Let them know you are paying attention. Don't drill your kid after a long day at school with questions such as:

"How did you do on your math quiz?"

This sounds like you are focusing mainly on their grades, often making a child feel extra pressure to succeed.

"Do you think that your teacher liked your presentation?"

"What grade do you think you will receive?"

"How did the other kids do on their presentations?"

Again, you are focusing on their grade, not the effort they put in.

"Do you think the teacher called on you enough, or did she call on the really smart kids again?"

You are starting with the assumption that the teacher is more interested in other kids, and you are clearly comparing your child to other students. This is never a good idea.

"Did you sit with Matty and Natalie today at lunch? Were they nice to you or did they exclude you from the conversation again? Did they talk only about themselves and not ask about you?"

Back off, Mom and Dad. Give your kids space to work out their own social interactions. Let them come to you with how they feel. Optimism is taught. Start with positive statements, and your child will follow your lead. Help your child to learn to see the positive in a situation. At the end of the day, take turns saying three things for which you are grateful.

"Did you hear there was another school shooting today? Many kids were shot and killed. I am so worried about you when you go to school. I pray this doesn't happen to you. I couldn't handle it if something happened to my baby!"

No, No, NO! Consider what is age-appropriate for you to share. Remember to give only as much information as is needed. When you show how worried you are about your children's safety, you are telling them they must really have something to worry about.

It takes practice to not drill your kids about their schoolwork, what they eat or didn't eat, and everything else you worry about, but pay attention to how you are thinking and feeling before you speak!

Scary times such as these demand you be creative, nurturing hope and forming a sacred space for your child to come to you for everything.

I won't deny I was a bit too anxious about my daughter's grades at times, and celebrated many of my kids' academic accomplishments or sports successes as if they won a Nobel Prize. However, I did try to find balance. I could be their biggest (and often loudest) cheerleader at swim meets, but I also could be a good listener.

Here are a few approaches to try when talking to your kids:

+ Share stories about your day.

+ Tell stories about some of your struggles and successes from your childhood.

+ Try not to be overly dramatic or too long-winded; try to keep each story to under three minutes in order to hold your child's attention.

+ Be patient.

+ Don't be afraid of some silence. Even if your child isn't speaking right after you tell a story or ask a question, it doesn't mean they aren't listening or thinking about it.

+ Don't make your child feel like he is the only important thing in your life. Generally speaking, if you just focus on what is happening in your childs' life, you may be putting too much pressure on them, creating self-absorbed, entitled kids.

+ Equally, don't make your child feel like you are over-burdened by her needs.

◆ Demonstrate that you get frightened by things, too. Talk about how you handle stressful situations, illustrating healthy self-care.

Use current events as a way to open up conversations, even if they are sometimes disturbing. Approach school violence in a calm but forthright way, keeping your child's emotional state front and center. For example, "Unfortunately, there was a school shooting today in (blank) town. Did you hear about it while you were in school?"

You also can ask your child if he or she ever worries about a particular student. You may ask, "Have you ever seen someone post something scary or threatening on social media?" or, "Do you see kids bully other kids?" Encourage your child to tell you if any other kids show "warning signs" or "red flag" behaviors.

"I Am Here"

When talking with your children, or with anyone in crisis or after a traumatic event, the best thing you can do is to tell them "I am here." This may sound simple or even a little silly, but it is one of the most powerful tools for helping another person. It literally lets that person know that he or she is not alone. This helps on an emotional level and allows the mind to switch off from crisis mode.

Several years ago, my mother was involved in a horrific motor vehicle accident. She was a passenger in a fourteen-seat van traveling to a social event. Besides her girlfriend, my mom did not know anyone in the van. Tragically, the driver of the van was moving too fast as he took a turn and smashed into a dump truck. The passenger side of the van took a direct hit. You guessed it. My mother was sitting in the front passenger seat. Her right arm was crushed in the door, every bone was broken, and she was losing a tremendous amount of blood. I still shake when I think of how close my mom came to losing her arm, dying from complications from several surgeries, or to death itself.

When the accident occurred, a woman sitting behind my mom jumped into action. She quickly helped my mother crawl over the driver's seat to get out, moving broken glass out of the way while never freaking out over the dire situation. She instructed others to help her get my mom to lie down on the ground, asking someone for a jacket, and then ripping an arm off it to make a tourniquet. She applied pressure on it to limit the bleeding as they waited for the police and ambulance to arrive. Another woman continued to hold my mother's good hand, leaning in to whisper in my mother's ear that she was going to be okay, that she wasn't going to die.

You may assume that these two brave women were professionals trained in emergency medicine or other crisis work, but they were both stay-at-home moms who acted out of kindness and love for a stranger.

Prior to my mom's accident, I thought I understood the power of positive thinking, but it was afterward that I became a passionate believer. Every-time my mother was about to be wheeled away on the stretcher for yet another surgery, I leaned down to kiss her forehead and whispered, "You will be fine." I also instructed the anesthesiologist to say those same words as she was putting my mother under. I strongly feel that if the patient is confident that he or she will be okay, outcomes can be much improved.

I believe that this same approach applies to children. It does not matter if it has to do with learning to socialize with friends, getting along with siblings, dealing with the stress of a big exam, or facing a life-or-death crisis. Regardless of the event or setting, showing positive support and compassion sends a powerful message and is a balm for the mind and body. That's always the way you should talk to your loved ones—especially your kids.

Talking About Lockdown Drills

As I've discussed throughout this book, short of an actual school incident involving violence, lockdown drills can be one of the scariest things your child will face.

In Melinda Sacks' *Stanford Magazine* article "Growing Up with School Lockdowns and Active Shooter Drills," she asks child psychiatrist Dr. Victor Carrion, "Is all this violence on school campuses having an impact on anxiety in children and families?"[1]

Dr. Carrion stresses that parents need to approach topics such as school violence in a "developmentally sensitive way."[2] She adds that "carrying out a drill in a vacuum can be stressful, but in the right context it can give children more confidence." It's not so much about having a drill or not having a drill, but how you are going to talk about it. How are you going to present it? It should be, "This is a safe environment and we will take care of you. This drill is part of that process." It is important for them to feel the adults have control.

When discussing lockdown drills in particular, keep these pointers in mind:

- Again, show your child that you are present. Convey that he is not alone.

- Take her hand, gently touch her face or give a hug. Whatever is your style is fine; just do something to let your child know you are present.

- Validate your child's feelings. Use "I" statements, such as, "I see that you are scared," "I'll bet it is scary during those lock down drills," or, "My heart would be beating fast while waiting for the drill to be over." Then, wait for an answer. If your child doesn't respond, just look in his eyes and nod like you get it; you understand.

- Be patient with your child. Remember it is about his experience, and not every detail of the drill that you personally may want to learn about.

- Be respectful of your child's feelings and thoughts. She may have opinions that are different from yours. Listen, discuss, and then help your child problem solve for the next time.

1,2 Melinda Sacks, "Growing Up with School Lockdowns and Active Shooter Drills," *Stanford Magazine*, April 4, 2018, https://medium.com/stanford-magazine/stanford-victor-carrion-on-active-shooter-drills-school-lockdowns-bd9f229b2549.

+ Watch for clues that your child wants to talk. Let his questions be your guide.

+ Don't judge your child's behavior

The Art of Being Calm

When discussing lockdown drills, you need to model calmness. If you show anxiety or hysteria by saying things such as, "I can't believe my baby has to hide in a dark corner of the classroom!" you are teaching your child to be fearful. If you act as if your child may get shot at any moment while he or she is in school, there is a very good chance that you will instill more fear. In order to make your child feel safe, you need to talk in a manner that displays confidence.

I reached out to a childhood friend who is a third-grade teacher and asked her about lockdowns and intruder drills from her particular perspective. She was grateful to have the opportunity to share her story and hoped it would help parents talk with their kids. Here's what she told me:

"I am a specialist teacher. I travel from one classroom to another. I was in the middle of teaching a lesson when we were interrupted by the announcement 'lockdown, lockdown.' I did what I've been instructed to do: I immediately walked to the door, locked it, and pulled down the shade. I then went to the windows to lower the blinds. Meanwhile, the children moved quickly and quietly to their designated hiding spaces. I joined them and we all sat in a tight huddle on the floor in the corner farthest from the door. I made eye contact with the children, nodding that we were all there, hopefully conveying that we were safe. Then we waited and waited.

"Some of the children started to look really worried. One child started to cry. Luckily, I found an illustrated book nearby, picked it up, and started silently telling the story as I turned page by page. It was a great distraction. We waited.

"It must have been over twenty minutes until there was a knock at the door. When I opened it, I was greeted by the principal's concerned

'Everything okay in here?' and was asked why I hadn't logged in on the computer to say we were all fine."

My friend explained that the protocol in her school was that once all the doors and windows were secure and the kids were in their hiding place, the teacher in charge was supposed to get on the classroom computer and email the principal that all was okay in their classroom. Due to the fact that she was a specialist, she did not know the code to log in. The main classroom teacher was absent, and no one had instructed the substitute teacher of the procedure. They realized the problem in the drill and worked toward fixing it. Meanwhile, twenty-three third graders sat huddled on the floor, thinking a shooter was in their building. My friend said that she, too, was getting concerned as the minutes ticked by.

I hope that the children left school, ate dinner with their moms and/or dads, and felt safe in their homes. I also hope that they had the words to share with their parents what it felt like to be scared. I hope their parents reminded them they were safe!

Coping Ahead to Better Manage Emotional Situations

Marsha Linehan, a psychologist who is the creator of Dialectical Behavior Therapy (DBT),[3] has done life-changing work with suicidal and/or borderline personality disorder clients. She created DBT to help treat the most difficult of clients, only to find it also works with children, adolescents, and adults suffering from depression and anxiety. The concept of using one's breath to help regulate emotions is key to DBT work.

As a student of DBT, as well as a clinician who incorporates it into my work, I find that what Marsha calls *coping ahead* to better manage emotional situations is a valuable tool that parents can use to help their

---

[3] "What Is Dialectical Behavioral Therapy (DBT)?" Behavioral Tech, https://behavioraltech.org/resources/faqs/dialectical-behavior-therapy-dbt/.

children deal with the threat of school gun violence. Part of Marsha's approach is a set of strategies she refers to as *emotion regulation*. It incorporates the following principles:

+ Accumulating positive emotions, both short- and long-term

+ Practicing building positive thoughts and emotions

+ Coping ahead to better manage emotional situations

This essentially means there are patterns to our behaviors and reactions that we can use to our advantage. We can use patterns from our past to try and cope ahead for when we encounter the same situation again later. It is by no means foolproof. It may work once, then may not work at another time, but there are definitely instances when it can help us, and when it does, it can feel like a lifesaver.

Coping ahead isn't about trying to guess the future. It's about knowing ourselves and the typical ways we have been triggered in the past. You can also call it mental preparation.

Coping ahead is a great skill to teach your children at every age. Lockdown drills and similar events can be frightening and upsetting to children and staff members. The goal is to teach everyone the idea of getting ahead of the anxiety in order to feel more in control.

Therefore, tell your children clearly and firmly that the principal and teachers have a plan for the drill. For example, "The teachers have practiced the drills before and they are there to keep you safe." Remind them that there is an extremely slim chance that anyone would come to their school to hurt them, but we can have a good plan just in case.

After an Incident

What if there's an actual incident in your town or anywhere else in the country? If you are constantly glued to the TV, watch every covered minute of a school shooting, have news alerts on your phone, or follow your favorite reporters on Twitter, there is a good chance you are too entrenched in the event. This is not beneficial for you or your children. Try to limit your child's exposure to the news during an actual event, in the aftermath of a tragic event, and even for months afterward.

Be honest and forthright about an incident, but base the amount of information you provide on the child's age. Remaining calm conveys to your child that you are in control, that it's okay to feel bad for others, and it's okay to express one's emotions. Also, let your child know that even though you are upset, you will continue to provide love, care, and protection. Remind your child that your family has a safety plan in case of emergencies. (For more information on this see Chapter 7, "Helping Your Kids Feel Safe with a Family Plan.")

Here are some useful guidelines to keep in mind when talking to your kids about violence in schools anywhere:

+ The most important step to take is to reassure them that they are physically safe.

+ Tell them that their schools are safe places.

+ Share with them that their teachers and principals are all trained to help keep them safe. Be specific: The school building is safe because the doors remain locked at all times. People entering the building have to ring a bell and then be authorized to get in. Many schools have cameras at all the doors that allow them to view any visitors.

Don't dismiss the power of your words. "You are safe and loved" goes a long way even if you only get a grunt or shrug from your kid. You may not see the impact of your words immediately, but my experience is that parenting is like planting a garden. We plant a lot of seeds by making positive comments, reinforcing positive behavior, and criticizing poor behavior but not the person. If you follow that approach, eventually good things will grow.

Talk About Guns

Whatever your view on gun laws in America, I am assuming that you do not want guns to get into the hands of unstable or violent people.

+ Talk to your kids about what to do if one of their friends' parents has a gun or guns. Do you permit your child to go over to that child's home? Do you call the parents, inquiring if they have guns in their home, and if so, where do they keep them?

+ Ask your child if he feels comfortable going over to a house where there are guns.

+ If you have a gun in your home, ask your child how she feels about it. Does it make her nervous, safe, or embarrassed to tell her friends?

+ Listen to what your child has to say. Acknowledge the courage it takes to share his thoughts with you. If you have a difference of opinion, see if you can come to a compromise that keeps him feeling safe.

During an interview with a fifteen-year-old young man about gun violence and school safety, he brought up the issue of his friend's parents having guns in their home. He said that he will not go over to anyone's house if he knows they have a gun. He said, "I just don't feel safe in someone's house if they have one."

It is important for parents to respect a child's judgment at certain times. This is one of those times. We need to teach our kids to trust their own instincts as well. This is a key ingredient for raising a confident, resourceful, self-reliant person.[4]

Talk Often

Make it a priority to talk with your children frequently about what is happening in school, and not just if they won their ball games or about their grades. Ask open-ended questions, and pay attention to their body language. Are they avoiding eye contact with you? Are they fidgeting more than usual? Or do they actually push back, stating something like "Mom, I said I don't want to talk about it." Respect their decision for

---

[4] "Talking to Children About Violence: Tips for Parents and Teachers," National Association of School Psychologists, https://www.nasponline.org/resources-and-publications/resources/school-safety-and-crisis/talking-to-children-about-violence-tips-for-parents-and-teachers.

now, but make sure you let them know they can always come to you with questions or concerns about school safety or violence. Set times for you and your child to do things together without technology that will promote dialogue and connection with each other.

Several times during an interview with a parent and child, the parent would answer a question saying, "No, my child is not worried about school shootings. They just know this is the reality we live in. I don't think it bothers them much." And then the child or teenager jumps in. "Mom, that is not true."

One twelve-year-old girl confided that she gets a little anxious, but she pretends that it doesn't bother her in front of her classmates.

Another tween told me that before the shooting in Parkland, some of the kids joked around during the drills, playing on their phones while others chatted with their friends. But now, things seem different. "I can tell that kids are more anxious during a lockdown drill," she said. "No one talks, and everyone seems to be waiting for the signal that the drill is over."

Parents need to be aware that they don't know how their children may feel during or after a school drill. It may depend on what type of drill was held or how the other kids reacted. Don't assume your child is fine. Ask them, and then listen.

Ask Age-Appropriate Questions

When discussing lockdown drills, actual incidents, or the general climate of fear that is out there, you should take the age of the child into account when you decide which questions you will ask your kids. Here are a few suggestions for determining those.

Kindergarten and Younger

+ If they have not heard about a school shooting, don't tell them.

+ If they have heard something, give them a one-line answer. Less is definitely more at this age. Always end with "you are safe."

+ Remind your child that it is extremely important to listen to his or her teachers. Give an example: "If the teacher says everyone must be quiet now, make sure you are quiet." Ask your child, "What does your teacher say when she wants the class to be quiet?"

+ Create a pattern of behavior so your child feels safe telling you when something at school makes her feel happy, sad, or confused.

+ Create a routine and talk about these kinds of issues at a regular designated time and place each day.

Ages 7 and 8

+ Ask your child what he heard. Listen to him.

+ Stay calm and answer directly. Four or five sentences is enough. Reinforce he is safe, using the general tips I provided above.

Ages 9 and Up

+ Ask open-ended questions such as, "I was wondering if there have been any lockdown drills in school lately?" Or, "Let me know when the drills happen in school, okay? Let's make sure we have time to talk about what happened during your drill."

+ Ask, "How did you feel when you first heard the announcement for the lockdown?"

+ "I was never in a lock down drill—what was it like to hide?"

+ "Do you think any of the other kids were upset? Why do you think so?"

Keep Communication Open

Remind your children that they can always talk to you about uncomfortable or upsetting things. Talk about the dangers of bullying on social media. It is okay to get upset with friends and classmates, but it is not okay to air their grievances on social media for the world to see. Remind them their brains are not fully developed yet; something that seems intolerable today may not feel so bad tomorrow.

Every parent should have a private code word or phrase that can be used when their kids need to communicate "help me." Come up with a word that you and your child can use in a text or post on social media if they need you to come pick them up.

I know many parents who have used this strategy with their middle school- and high school-aged children. Just imagine you drop your fifteen-year-old daughter and her friends off at another girl's home. They tell you that the parents are home and only a few other girls are coming over. It turns out the girl who was hosting the gathering didn't tell her parents she was having a lot of kids over. The parents thought only a few girls were coming over. They went out to dinner locally, thinking it was okay to leave them alone. Thanks to the magic of the internet, word got out fast that there was a party at their home.

Luckily, you and your daughter have a plan and code phrase for unplanned situations. You receive a text: "Pie, please. I need pie now!" You don't start texting her questions, "Are you sure you want to come home? Is everything okay?"

Go get her. *Then* ask questions. Honor her decision to leave what feels like an unsafe situation. This is paramount to your daughter trusting you. It also helps your daughter build a sense of decision-making ability, judgment, and self-respect. You respect her judgment, thus she is learning how to trust it as well.

Don't Tell Your Kid You Are a Cool Parent

I start hearing parents refer to their kids as "cool" by the time they are in preschool. More than that, I often hear parents tell their kids that they have cool parents. Stop doing this, please!

What does it mean to have a "cool" parent? Does that mean if parents are "cool," their kids have to be "cool," too? This is only adding pressure on our children.

In November 2014, educator and writer Andrew Reiner published an article in *The Washington Post* titled "Parents, You Are Not Doing

Your Kids Any Favors by Being 'Cool.'" He notes that for all too many parents, a big part of being "cool" today means curating a Photoshop-perfect image on social media, staying constantly looped into whatever pop culture news has gone viral, and blithely dropping pithy, snarky tweets and text messages—as if this was the way we talk all of the time. In other words, you're cool if you're relevant.[5]

Reiner went on to write that both parents and kids are adjusting, modifying their views and images based upon what they think others will approve of or "like." He goes on to note that the pressure to be "on" in your social devices all the time—to look perfect all the time—is proving to be too much for many of our young people.

Reiner also stated that we do our children an epic disservice by modeling behavior that hurts them in the long run, sometimes with tragic consequences. If we want to do right by our children, then instead of "being cool," we should "cool it."[6] He makes an important point that many of his college students are too quick to go with the "majority think," often stating that they "agree completely" with the person who spoke before them.

I read this article, noting that it was written in 2014, and thought of how much worse things have become for our kids and adults. This makes your job that much more critical. In addition, my concern is that this puts a stumbling block in the way of your children feeling comfortable talking to you about their feelings of drills or other issues that are upsetting them.

Recommendations for Schools

Most children spend about six hours per day in school, and during the week see their teachers more than their own parents. Given that and the sad fact that schools these days increasingly are the epicenter of violence

[5,6] Andrew Reiner, "Parents, You Are Not Doing Your Kids Any Favors by Being 'Cool.'" *The Washington Post*, November 21, 2014, https://www.washingtonpost.com/news/parenting/wp/2014/11/21/parents-youre-not-doing-your-kids-any-favors-by-being-cool/?utm_term=.5c6538045034.

against children, here a few recommendations for how school personnel can approach talking to kids about gun violence, and lockdown drills in particular:

1. **Send an email to the parents when a lockdown, intruder, and/or evacuation drill occurred, informing them a drill was held that day.** In my interviews, I only came across a few school districts that did this.

2. **Encourage parents to talk to their kids about the school drills.** Provide a series of conversation starters for the parents to use. Be aware that some schools use words such as, "lockdown drill," "code red," "code yellow," or "lockdown in place." Ask kids to explain what each one is. Ask if they ever forget what they are supposed to be doing and if that frightens them. Use "I" statements such as, "I can imagine that can be confusing. One minute you are learning history or science, and the next you are figuring out if you have to hide under your desk or just say quiet in place." Keep in mind that some of the newer drills that schools have been incorporating allow the students and teacher of each classroom to decide if it is a safer choice to hide or try to escape the building.

3. **Create a one-page flyer or email blast to send out to students and their parents.** In it, provide a list of local community service organizations. Research supports the concept that it is beneficial for families to do things together, and both children and adults feel better when they are involved in community service activities and when they are helping other people.

4. **Provide parenting education forums on the topic of talking to your kids in this climate of fear.** This provides parents an opportunity to voice their concerns, learn from the administration and the police of school safety procedures, and even learn techniques on managing their own fears and those of their children.

5. **Help teachers deal with lockdown drills.** Most parents understand that it is a huge responsibility to be a teacher. They

are now expected to teach their students *and* protect them from guns. Schools districts need to provide teachers with adequate training to not only implement safe lockdown drills, but to help their students deal with the emotional components of the drills.

It isn't uncommon for some kids, especially in the younger grades, to have adverse reactions to the drills. Many students have told me they've seen other kids get really upset during the drills. How is a teacher supposed to comfort an upset student, or figure out if the lockdown drill is a just that or the real thing, all the while keeping an eye on the other students? Schools need to have educational workshops to assist their staff in appropriate strategies to deal with the children's emotions as well as providing them with a chance to explore their feelings.

The Continuing Conversation

Here is some additional food for thought about talking with your kids about gun violence:

- Don't meddle too much in their lives—especially if they are in high school. They want to learn how to live independently, so try to limit giving your opinion to when it is asked for.

- Show respect and you may receive it back. We all react better when we are respected.

- Don't say, "I told you so." Support them when they fail. Help them figure out why this situation happened and what could they do differently next time.

- Don't break their confidence by telling your friends about their latest struggles. Somehow, kids always know when you do this.

- Don't be too dramatic. It isn't the end of the world.

- Learn to be a good role model. Behavior speaks volumes.

- Stay current. Know what is trending with kids and teens.

- Find a non-violent show you can watch with your kids.

- Have a "date" once in a while with your child.

+ Set up a social media contract with your child that includes you monitoring your child's exposure to violent content.

+ See if your pediatrician is willing to talk to you and your kids about their "media diets."[7]

+ Play with your kid. Know what games your child is playing and play with them. Create one night as "Game Night."

+ Children under the age of six should not be allowed to play or watch violence. Young children cannot always tell the difference between what is real and what is fantasy.

+ Talk to your children about the scientific connection between virtual violence and real-life aggression.[8]

+ Help your child play without a screen in front of him or her. Encourage creative hobbies as well as physical ones.

+ Create time for unstructured play and down time.

I asked a group of parents, "Do your kids talk about being scared to go to school because of school shootings?" I couldn't even finish my question before many jumped in declaring, "Yes!" One mom said, "My daughter talks about it all the time." Another added that she worries that it is becoming a bigger problem this year for her child.

A mother told me that there was a lockdown drill in her daughter's elementary school recently. When she picked up her daughter after school, she went on and on about having to hide in the closet during a drill. The mom did not know that it was an unscheduled drill. Unfortunately, she thought her daughter was being overly dramatic. She told her to stop making such a big deal about it, stating "You have drills all the time." It was only later that evening that she received an email from the school alerting parents that a teacher had taken very ill and they

---

[7] "Virtual Violence," American Academy of Pediatrics, August, 2016, http://pediatrics.aappublications.org/content/early/2016/07/14/peds.2016-1298.

[8] https://www.nih.gov/news-events/news-releases/abcd-study-completes-enrollment-announces-opportunities-scientific-engagement

needed to keep the children confined while they got the teacher safely out of the building.

Take the extra time to listen to your children, acknowledge them, and then validate their experiences. Even if this had been a typical lockdown drill, you need to meet your child where she is. Listen for the "Why is my child talking about this situation?" clues. Then you will be better prepared to help her talk about her fear, process her feelings, and even problem-solve how she can best take of herself next time.

Remember that you are your child's role model. When situations arise that are frightening, model calmness. Most importantly, don't act as if talking about scary and even violent things are taboo. Avoidance only adds to a child feeling scared and unsafe.

Remind your children that as frightening and annoying as lockdown drills may be, they are part of the system that is in place to keep them safe. Above all, remind your kids that they are safe at home and at school, and that there are many adults whose job is to protect them.

CHAPTER 6

Strategies to Help
Your Child (and You) Cope

"Mindfulness means paying attention in a particular way: on purpose, in the present moment, and nonjudgmentally." – Jon Kabat-Zinn

"Mindfulness shows us what is happening in our bodies, our emotions, our minds, and in the world. Through mindfulness, we avoid harming ourselves and others." – Thich Nhat Hanh

I was sitting in a circle on a rubber alphabet mat, surrounded by a small group of kindergarteners in a mini-class called Quiet Time. It was the early 2000s. I was teaching children meditation and mindfulness techniques that had not yet become mainstream in U.S. schools.

A forward-thinking private school welcomed my idea of trying to teach children the value of being quiet and some basic breathing techniques. During class one day, a little girl raised her hand and said that sometimes her mom tells her to be quiet, put on her headphones, don't talk, and listen to her music.

Oh no, I remember thinking, that can't be good for kids to learn, even if it is an effective way for a mom to get some sort of peace.

During class I had all the kids lie back, close their eyes, and listen to their breath. I remember telling them a guided story that helped them pay attention to different sensations in their body and visualize images in their minds. I kept the exercise to ten minutes. The kids seemed to really like it, returning to class calmer, and I would bet, more focused.

Mindfulness is our capacity to put our awareness where we want it. Do I put my thoughts on how much homework I have to do when I get home? Do I continue to worry about whether my school may get shot up, or do I redirect my thoughts back to my breath?

Now more than ever, there is a tremendous need for children to learn how to regulate their thoughts and breath in an effort to feel a sense of calm. I always urge parents and teachers alike to bring a sense of stillness and inner peace into their children's lives. Mindfulness is a powerful tool that can help them learn to modulate their feelings and master a sense of control over their thoughts, including fears about lockdown drills and school shootings, as well as the many other challenges that life throws their way. Mindfulness is an incredibly important technique that helps children prepare, cope, and feel safe in today's violent environment.

An Antidote to Stress

Jon Kabat-Zinn, credited as a pioneer in bringing a meditative approach to treating pain, stress, and depression to his patients at the University of Massachusetts Medical School in 1976, has stated, "Mindfulness is basically just a particular way of paying attention, and the awareness that arises through paying attention in that way. It is a way of looking deeply into oneself in the spirit of self-inquiry and self-understanding."[1] Another way to look at mindfulness is to pay attention to your breath, then pay attention to your breath going in and out of your nose. Just pay attention to that sensation. What is happening? What do you feel? What do you see? What do you hear?

Kabat-Zinn also has noted that "mindfulness is the art of non-doing. Not doing, stretching into a moment's enormity, is a way to grow into ourselves. And this will serve our children, not only ourselves. When we model mindfulness, not just attempt to enter the moment

---

[1] Jon Kabat-Zinn, *Full Catastrophe Living: Using the Wisdom of Your Body and Mind to Face Stress, Pain, and Illness*, (New York: Bantam Books, 1990).

our children observe, but when we find our own moment, we may be the most helpful."[2]

A Day to Remember

I first started teaching meditation to children years ago. I was working as a therapist at a Jewish overnight camp in the Berkshires. It was a special place for me: I attended overnight camp there as a child, worked there in my late teens, and returned in my late twenties with a masters in social work, a husband, and two babies all packed into my Volvo station wagon. I loved camp. It was a place where I felt safe to grow, heal, and help others.

One day, a rabbi who was leading an afternoon workshop on spirituality and meditation for kids forgot to show up. Rebecca, the education director, handed me a book on Judaism and meditation and asked if I could teach the class. There was a group of teens hanging out under my favorite tree. (I used to sit under this tree and dream when I was a camper. It was huge, with one branch that seemed to reach up to the sky.)

I suppose you could say I used to mediate, so this assignment really resonated with me. Having the opportunity to teach this class opened a new door for me and proved to be a pivotal moment in my life.

I joined the kids under the tree, quickly selected a page in the meditation book, and went with it. I remember the meditation as if it was yesterday. I still can feel the breeze as it brushed my body, the birds chirping in the distance, the brilliant blue skies shining over the Berkshire Mountains. I can even clearly recall two of my students, and I can recite that mediation right now, word by word.

It was in the stillness of the air, watching the campers lie peacefully in the shade, that I could almost see how the world slows down when we become more peaceful. At that moment, it became so clear to me that

---

[2] Wendy Sue Swanson, "Mindful Parenting," Seattle Children's Hospital, January 25, 2013, https://seattlemamadoc.seattlechildrens.org/mindful-parenting.

one of the most significant things children, well let's be real, *all of us* need, is the ability to quiet our minds and bodies in order to feel safe.

The students and counselors seemed to be impacted by the meditation. They said that they felt so relaxed. A few of the students said they never experienced such closeness with nature. One even said that it was extremely spiritual.

I watched the kids' reactions, I listened to their words describe their experiences, and I surrendered to the feeling of being present in the moment. It was liberating to know that I could help people relax through the power of my words and my energy.

Why was that meditation class so memorable for me? Perhaps because it was the day I fully realized how powerful words, intention, energy, and setting can be on the body and the soul.

Since then, I have incorporated many different types of meditation and breathing techniques in sessions with my clients and students. I became a dedicated student of mindfulness and meditation, studying with many gifted teachers.

In light of the ever-increasing stress and fear that so many kids report, mindfulness can be extremely helpful and healing not just for children, but for the adults in their lives as well.

The Benefits of Being Calm

It is critical for parents, teachers, and schools districts to prioritize teaching mindfulness techniques to children. As the adults in our children's world continue to figure out the best methods and strategies to keep them safe, the time to teach mindfulness methods is now.

The benefits of teaching your child mindfulness and meditation techniques include:

+ Less anxiety

+ Reduced stress

+ Increased focus

+ More confidence

+ Enhanced creativity

+ A better sense of balance

+ Improved relaxation

+ Better sleep

Role Model Your Calm

Hysteria, paralyzing fear, and hyper-sensitivity to external stimuli happen for a reason but can be avoided. As I noted previously, being glued to news coverage of a school shooting is a good example of being too entrenched in the event. This is not beneficial for you or your children. You need to stop what you are doing, look directly into their eyes, and pay attention to what you see, speaking to them in a manner that displays confidence. This lets them know that you are in control and that you have a plan, which means they will have a plan to keep them safe. Learn this simple mindfulness technique and practice it with your children. It is a good thing to do as part of their bedtime ritual.

**"In mindfulness, one is not only restful and happy but alert and awake. Meditation is not evasion; it is a serene encounter with reality."
– Thich Nhat Hanh[3]**

The Power of Breathing

Thich Nhat Hanh, a Buddhist monk and peace activist, offers this short mindful meditation in his book *Being Peace*: "Breathing in, I calm my body. Breathing out, I smile. Dwelling in the present moment, I know this is a wonderful moment."

---

[3] Thich Nhat Hanh, *The Miracle of Mindfulness An Introduction to the Practice of Meditation*, (Boston, Mass: Beacon Press, 2016).

In another book, *Miracle of Mindfulness: An Introduction to the Practice of Meditation*, Thich Nhat Hanh teaches people to learn practical techniques and stimulating ways to live life. He shares how he was sitting with a friend who was telling him a story while peeling and eating a tangerine. The friend was so immersed in the story that he was not conscious of putting segments of the tangerine into his mouth. He wasn't aware that his mouth was full and that he hadn't started to chew the previous segments that had previously plopped in there.

How many of us do not eat consciously, such as by eating our food while binge-watching a favorite Netflix show, or even while driving on the highway at eighty miles an hour? Thich Nhat Hanh uses this story as a description of how distracted we can become when we aren't present in the details of our life.

This story resonates with me because I believe that many parents are so focused on their goals and dreams for their children that they aren't enjoying the journey. If you are focused on the next achievement, for example, "Will my child make the traveling soccer team?" or, "Will she get into AP classes?" or, "Will being involved in a certain club look good on his college application?", you're most likely not only putting pressure on your child, but are also missing out on everyday joy.

Additionally, consider whether you are teaching your child to live for external accomplishments—feeling good, satisfied, and proud—only when they reach the finish line and accomplishes tasks. A tremendous void may be created by not teaching them to learn to find purpose, enjoyment, contentment, and satisfaction along the way.

Connecting with the Body

Children being raised by the internet, from which they consume an over-abundance of information via their electronic devices, has created enormous deficits. One is that children and young adults are disconnected from their bodies in a way we have never seen before. Kids spend so much of their time on the internet or in an alternative gaming world that it results in a huge disconnect between what is happening in their body and their awareness of the connection to their thoughts and feelings.

In addition, many children, especially teens, don't move much during a typical day, which adds to the sense of feeling disconnected. When you move your body in dance, running, or even walking, it serves to ground you.

Any form of mindful activity, such as yoga, meditation, or even taking a walk without being plugged in to a device, is a *huge* step toward helping children begin the process of learning to connect to their body and be still within themselves.

Lots of schools, gyms, community centers, and commercial studios offer yoga classes for children and teens. There are even classes that parents can take with their children. If yoga doesn't fit your family's needs, try some form of martial arts or another exercise. Encourage your child to take regular walks or runs.

Non-Negotiables

I advise parents to have some non-negotiable, required activities. From a young age in our home, my husband and I understood that learning physical skills such as dance, swim, karate, and even yoga would become part of our children's foundation. It is never too late to start having some non-negotiables.

How are we preparing children to be physically and emotionally fit to handle various scenarios of lockdown drills and possible school shootings? From my personal research, I don't think we are doing very well preparing them in either way.

Breathing Buddies

Dr. Daniel Goleman, psychologist, speaker, and author of the book, *Emotional Intelligence*, discounts IQ as the sole measure of one's abilities. That book was an enormous success and is a must-read for all parents. Dr. Goleman is one of the leading experts on meditation, promoting the benefits of mindfulness practice in the everyday lives of children and adults. He believes that doing ten minutes of meditation three times a day, every day, can improve your attention, lower stress levels, and help calm the mind to face the challenges of life.

Dr. Goleman teaches that one of the ways children can learn better and improve their concentration is with "Breathing Buddies," a technique in which they use their breath to calm themselves down. The Breathing Buddy is a stuffed animal, toy, or even a favorite rock. They can lie down on their bed, or if in a classroom, on the floor. They put their Breathing Buddy on their stomach as they take in deep breaths in for a count of three, keeping their eyes on their buddy on their tummy. Then they exhale for a count of three. They watch their buddy go up *one, two, three*, and down *one, two, three*. This is training the child's mind to stay focused on his or her body. This technique will help your kid focus on what the teacher is saying and will make it easier to manage distressing emotions in his or her life. It is an inner, self-management training that uses basic repetition to help train the mind. According to Dr. Goleman, "This simple exercise strengthens the brain's circuits for attention. The prefrontal circuitry that focuses the mind also calms the body from stress arousal, training the child's brain to be able to recover more quickly from upsetting emotions."[4]

This is a fabulous technique to use with preschoolers as well as high school students. For the older children, instead of using stuffed animals, you can have them visualize an apple or a shell sitting on top of their bellies.

It is always helpful when learning to do these kinds of breathing exercises to remember that it is normal for your mind to wander, just remember to bring it back to your breath.

---

[4] Daniel Goleman, "Focus, Social and emotional learning," October 15, 2013, http://www.danielgoleman. info/focus-changed-thinking-emotional-intelligence/.

A Breathing Meditation

Try three ten-minute sessions of mindfulness throughout the day. Put everything aside for the time being, and bring your full attention to your breath. Don't try to control it—just focus on the full in-breath and the full out-breath. If you notice that your mind has wandered, simply bring it back to your breathing and start over with the next breath.

Don't judge yourself for your runaway thoughts—we all have them. When you start a mindfulness practice you become hyper-aware of how much your mind wanders away from what you are trying to concentrate on. But it's the act of bringing the focus back to the breath that seems to strengthen the brain's circuitry for concentration.

Children and even teens are often more open to learning and utilizing mindfulness techniques. They may act like it is not for them, not cool, or too weird, but once you can get them enthused, it can be a welcome break in their stressful lives.

Creating a Safe Place for Expression

Serena is a yoga teacher who has been teaching at-risk children in an urban city for years. In that environment, many children are taught to keep their emotions to themselves and not to show how they are truly feeling. This is completely at odds with what children need. When Serena is brought into a classroom, she creates a safe place where children can allow their emotions to flow through movement, yoga poses, dance, howling, and laughter. She teaches them how to use their breath as a way to connect with their bodies and to learn to feel a sense of control. She adds that, despite the fact that the kids are dealing with many economic and emotional challenges, they all listen and participate.

Serena explained that one day, a young boy, age six, was sitting on the floor while trying to put on his sneaker. The other students had already put their shoes on and were off to lunch. He was crying hard as he continued to try to jam his too-large foot into an old sneaker. Realizing what the problem was, she sat down on the floor with him and instructed him to start using his breathing skills.

"Take a deep breath in, hold for three seconds, and release for three seconds," she suggested. He started taking deep breaths, quickly calming down. He then put his foot in the shoe, giving Serena a little smile.

There is nothing better than giving children skills to help them learn to regulate their emotions in order to calm down.

Teens Need to Meditate, Too

Many years ago, I spent hours sitting in the dark on the *bima* (stage) in my synagogue, leading a class on spirituality and meditation for high school juniors and seniors. The only light in the sanctuary was the warm glow from the *ner tamid*, the "eternal flame" that hangs in every synagogue, right above the holy ark, the home of the Torah scrolls. I had my students lie down on the floor with their heads facing up to the *ner tamid*. We would talk about God, what God is, what is the meaning of life, what is death, what happens to the soul when someone dies, reincarnation, and everything else.

On many of those evenings, my students would open their minds, their hearts, and to me, what felt like their souls, as they shared their ideas and fears.

Every class started with me leading a meditation to help get them in the mood. I created a sacred space for them to breathe, to become comfortable with being quiet with themselves, and to relax. Following the meditation, we would talk.

One night after class, a young man came up to me and said, "Thanks for class tonight. I don't know if I understand what happened to me during the meditation. I felt warm, I felt calm, and I felt so relaxed." We talked for a few minutes about his experience. I believe I helped create a space for him to safely, and without judgment, explore his spirituality, open up his mind in a new way, and most of all, just learn to quiet his mind.

Practicing Mindfulness During Lockdown Drills

Practicing meditation and mindfulness can go a long way toward helping your child be comfortable during the stressful experience of a lockdown drill. As I discussed earlier in the book, sometimes teachers will give their students a heads-up about an impending drill because they know how scary it can be for kids. However, all too often, they do not know if it is a drill or the real thing as they run for safety.

As soon as the principal's voice comes over the loudspeaker, the child's brain launches into action. The mind goes into *fight or flight* mode when stress, especially intense stress, occurs. Teach your child to pay attention to his or her thoughts and then the physical reactions in his or her body. Is his stomach feeling queasy? Are her neck muscles or back tightening up? Are there other physical symptoms? Help your child make the connection between having worrying thoughts and feeling distress in the body. Tell your child to take deep breaths, put a hand on her chest, or cross her arms as if giving herself a big hug. This can be very comforting.

The key is to always acknowledge that your child is feeling some form of distress. Talk frankly with your kids about this. Listen to what they are saying. Direct their thoughts to how their bodies feel after they give themselves a hug or put their hands on their chests. Usually, bringing one's attention to what the physical body is feeling regulates and can even slow down the overactive mind.

Breathing Exercises During Lockdown Drills

Most parents have never experienced the type of lockdown drills that kids are enduring today. With compassion and understanding, suggest to your children that when they are waiting to find out if the event is a drill or a real emergency, there is something very powerful they can do with their thoughts. They can become mindful using the Breathing Buddies exercise, as Dr. Goleman teaches, or they can do any other form of breathing or meditation. This will help them keep their minds calm and clear, although they also should always keep their eyes open during the drills!

Other Resources for Learning How to Be Mindful

Together, you and your kids can learn a variety of different mediation and breathing techniques. Many yoga, exercise, or even school gym classes teach kids different styles of meditation these days, and you also can check YouTube for suggestions on kid- or teen-friendly meditations.

Additionally, there are a number of apps that can help with guided meditations, calming music, and sounds. I am familiar with "*Calm*," "*The Mindfulness App*," and "*Headspace*," but there are many more available.

Make an activity out of it—go searching for different apps with your kids. Try some out and see what you think.

Another Breathing Mediation

Take three deep breaths. Breathe in slowly and breathe out with a loud sigh. Imagine that you are filling up a big blue balloon with your breath. The blue balloon is in your stomach. Take deep breaths, filling up your belly. Then slowly release your breath. Repeat at least three times.

As you continue doing the deep breathing, imagine you are standing in your favorite place—maybe the beach—and immerse yourself in it. Imagine you can hear the sounds of the ocean waves breaking on the sand. You hear the birds in the distance, you can see the exquisite blue sky, feel the breeze as it whispers across your skin. Imagine you can taste the salty air, and feel how your body relaxes. Continue to enjoy this peaceful place, and continue taking deep breaths.

Teach your child to do this little exercise whenever and wherever he or she is feeling stressed or impatient, including during lockdown drills.

Walk the Talk

Make time each day for yourself. It is important to find time, even if it's only ten minutes, to do something restorative. Set times for you and your child to practice meditations together. It is a great thing to do before bed, helping the body to relax and unwind. Share stories with your child of times you have chosen to meditate. Give examples of some of the benefits you experienced.

Remember that there is no right or wrong way to do it!

Often I will hear my students or clients state, "I can't sit still; I can't mediate," or, "Are you kidding me? There is so much noise inside my head, I can't mediate."

This is why it is so important to do the breathing techniques. It will literally train your brain to learn to be more focused and disciplined.

"I always get distracted by my own thoughts!" Acknowledge the thoughts and then redirect your mind back to taking three deep breaths in and exhaling three deep breaths out.

One of my favorite responses to this is: "It is okay if your mind starts to wonder, if you lose focus. Simply take a few deep cleaning breaths and redirect your mind back to the sound of my voice."

This is a simple yet very powerful statement. It strives to acknowledge the person's experience while still giving them tools to refocus on the meditation.

Expand Your Knowledge and Experience

Take long walks on the beach, focusing on the sound of water crashing on the shore. Take a walk or a hike in the woods, allowing your mind to let go of all the external noises and focus on the beauty around you.

Do some research! There are many wonderful mindful meditation teachers available. Read books on mediation, listen to powerful podcasts on your phone, find someone who speaks to your heart and go for it. Take a step outside your comfort zone.

Today, it is becoming almost mainstream to learn and develop your own inner health fitness plan including nutritional support, yoga practices, and meditation.

I am excited to see the Western medical community embracing the ideas of meditation into its practices. According to the *Journal of the American Medical Association (JAMA)*, clinicians should be aware that meditation programs can result in small to moderate reductions of multiple negative dimensions of psychological stress.[5]

Dr. Elizabeth Hoge, a psychiatrist at the Center for Anxiety and Traumatic Stress Disorders at Massachusetts General Hospital and an assistant professor of psychiatry at Harvard Medical School, says that mindfulness meditation makes perfect sense for treating anxiety. "People with anxiety have a problem dealing with distracting thoughts that have too much power," she explains. "They can't distinguish between a problem-solving thought and a nagging worry that has no benefit."[6]

When working with clients suffering with anxiety and depression,

---

[5] Madhav Goyal, "Meditation Programs for Psychological Stress and Well-being," JAMA Network, March, 2014, https://jamanetwork.com/journals/jamainternalmedicine/fullarticle/1809754.

[6] Julie Corliss, "Mindfulness Meditation May Ease Anxiety, Mental Stress," Harvard Health Publishing, January 8, 2014, https://www.health.harvard.edu/blog/mindfulness-meditation-may-ease-anxiety-mental-stress-201401086967.

I often teach them to pay attention to their thoughts or to their "self-talk." Self-talk is our inner dialogue that is a critical component of an individual's mind. The problem is when a person's self-talk becomes too loud, too assertive, it becomes a challenge for the individual to manage. I sometimes refer to the thoughts as runaway ideas that can spin out of control into a large ball.

Meditation practice can successfully help a person learn to identify when runaway thoughts are being generated and how to tame them.

Appreciate the Moment

Mindfulness, meditation, walking, and yoga are all helpful things to do to keep us healthy and present. In times of stress and uncertainty, these things can help both children and adults deal with emotions, stress, and depression.

In his book, *Everyday Blessings: The Inner Work of Mindful Parenting*, Jon Kabat-Zinn says that it is a parent's job to "nurture, protect, and guide our children and bring them along until they are ready to walk their own paths." He adds that parents also "need to continue growing and developing ourselves—each of us in our way . . . Mindful parenting is hard work. It means getting to know ourselves inwardly, and working at the interface where our lives meet the lives of our children. It is particularly hard work in this era when the culture is intruding more and more into our homes and into our children's lives, and attention spans are becoming shorter and shorter and our minds more and more distracted."

Think of the moments a child takes in and absorbs each day, and how he or she helps you to see the world differently. Parenting is a privilege, and having these little teachers around us is true wealth, but it's not necessarily easy. Our children will teach us about mindfulness naturally, but we'll likely be startled to learn that while we think the curriculum is one thing, repeatedly they'll demonstrate it's something totally different.

I hope this chapter encourages you to learn more about mindfulness, meditation, and yoga or another way to create a few minutes of peace and grounding in this age of school violence. After you finish reading this, I challenge you to put the book down, close your eyes, and try out the breathing techniques I've discussed.

Feel your feet on the ground, your back up against the chair, the air going in and out of your body. Then open your eyes.

Short meditation helps you remember that no matter what is going on, you and your children have the ability to stop, breathe, and re-center yourselves. Remember that this practice helps children learn to recover quicker after a stressful situation, making them more resilient and resourceful.

CHAPTER 7

Helping Your Kids Feel Safe with a Family Plan

If there was a school emergency tomorrow, would you have a plan? What if there was a school shooting and you had no way to contact your kids? The best way to protect your family is to have a safety plan. Talking to your children about the need for a safety plan will make them feel more comfortable and secure.

I have spoken with numerous families who admitted they did not have a safety plan. They also said they had not spoken directly about safety issues with their children! I have heard many excuses including, "We are so busy," and, "We just haven't gotten around to it, though it's on our to-do list," or, "We have talked about what we would do if there was a flood or an earthquake." The most prevalent reason for not having this discussion seems to be that parents are concerned that if they talk to their kids about scary things, such as a school shooting or a natural disaster, they will frighten them.

Don't be naive. Today's children have been exposed to an excess of inappropriate information for their age. This includes endless hours of playing violent video games, overhearing Mom and Dad talk about the news, pictures in the newspaper, or images that appear on their social media sites. Consequently, many kids already live with a lot of fear ranging from natural disasters and terrorist attacks, to (of course), school shootings. Talking with them in a structured, forthright manner can only help. In fact, talking to them about a safety plan may be one of the most important discussions you have.

Putting Together Your Plan

A family safety plan begins with holding a "family meeting." Select a designated time for your family to come together to discuss a safety plan for emergencies. Specifically discuss what to do if something happens during school hours. Go over school emergency procedures.

Be prepared with your laptop and phone to document your ideas. Set the goal of having a complete step-by-step guide for what each family member is to do in a variety of potential crisis situations.

Here are some sample conversation starters:

"We are going to talk about some things that may make you feel uncomfortable or even a bit scared. Hopefully, we will never have to use this information, but we need to talk about it."

"You know how you have lockdown drills and fire drills at school? The principal and the teachers practice with you to make sure you are prepared in case of an emergency. We are going to do the same thing."

"What would you do if . . .?"

Create a list of questions for your kids to answer. Don't make it scary. Tell them that an incident is unlikely, but *if* something were to happen, they should know what to do.

Your family safety plan should be based on different scenarios, such as "What if Mom and Dad aren't home from work before the kids get home?" Ready.gov has created a complete set of instructions for parents to discuss with their families. Take a look at the plan below. Depending on the ages of your children, decide which of the following components are appropriate[1]:

- **Set a general meeting place.** Decide on a general meeting place if one or more of you cannot make it home or to the school.

- **Create an emergency backpack.** A great idea one mom shared with me was to have an "emergency backpack" ready in case of an unexpected event. In the backpack is a piece of paper with everyone's contact and insurance information, a flashlight, protein bars, and assorted other things she thought her family might need.

---

[1] https://www.ready.gov

Some parents have shared that they put a stuffed animal or small toy, crayons in effort to comfort children. Add a pair of socks and undies for each person just in case you have to spend the night somewhere unexpectedly.

+ **Set up an alert system.** Enable your phone to receive alerts and warnings from local police. Go to the police website or call them to find out how to receive alerts on your electronic devices. FEMA has an Integrated Public Alert and Warning System (IPAWS). Go to https://www.fema.gov/media-library/assets/videos/77356 to learn more and to sign up to receive alerts.

+ **Compile a list of emergency numbers.** Compile a list of all emergency phone numbers. These should include parents' work and cell numbers and the cellphone numbers of each of your children. Also note the numbers of friends and neighbors in case of an emergency. Write all the numbers on a piece of paper or type them up and print them out in case you can't access electronic devices. Put all the important papers in a safe place. Share with your kids who is on the list and why they are included, then:

  - Put the list in a place that is known and available to all family members.

  - Put it in everyone's phone.

  - Email the list to a trusted friend or family member not living in your home.

+ **Talk about what to do if there is a shooting in a nearby school or another type of emergency.** Initiate this conversation with your child in a calm manner. Plan ahead so you know what your mission is and how you can get there. Leave time for your child to ask questions. Again, be patient and stay silent for a bit. Let your child absorb the information and think about how he or she is feeling.

+ **Have a social media plan. If cell service is down, plan to go to Facebook, Snapchat, or Instagram for information.** Social media sites can be very effective in times of crisis. During the school shooting at Marjorie Stoneman Douglas High School, many families were able to get the word out that their children were safe by posting on Facebook and Snapchat.

+ **Learn about the types of natural disasters that may affect your community.** Discuss this with your children in a matter-of-fact style. Come up with several plans of how you would evacuate if the need ever arose. Become familiar with shelters in your area, and if you have pets, check to see if the shelter will accept them.

+ **Go to the FEMA website and print out the family emergency communication plan.**[2] Fill it out and store in a safe place.

Keep an Emergency Kit in Your Car

It's a good idea to keep a small emergency kit in your car. You can buy one at your local drugstore. These usually contain antibacterial wash and cream, bandages, eye wash, and a pain reliever. Also include the following with your emergency supplies:

- Flashlight
- Jumper cables
- Flares or reflective triangles
- Car cell phone charger

"Stop the Bleed" and Other Programs

During a conversation with Pam, a first responder from Parkland, she alerted me to a program called "Stop the Bleed,"[3] created by the U.S. Department of Homeland Security, that had been presented to her community. This program is intended to help bystanders assist in a bleeding emergency before professional help arrives. No matter how rapid the arrival of professional emergency responders, bystanders will always

---

[2] https://www.fema.gov/media-library-data/1501681925535-41606db2566a70a863290fafd475a2a2/Family_Communication_Plan_Fillable_Card_508.pdf

[3] https://www.dhs.gov/stopthebleed

be first on the scene. A person who is bleeding can die from blood loss within five minutes; therefore, it is important to take action immediately. Those nearest to someone with life-threatening injuries are best positioned to provide first care.

Pam told me that over 200 members of the greater area surrounding Parkland signed up for the "Stop the Bleed" class. She reported that many teachers and parents took it because they were worried that they would not know what to do if someone was shot or injured and bleeding severely.

I am not recommending that teens take this class, but I think it is important for you to know that it is available. Just stop for a minute and think about the enormity of this situation. Are we telling students and teachers that their schools are so dangerous that there may be a time they will need to know how to stop a friend or a teacher from bleeding to death from a gunshot wound? Or, are you saying that accidents can happen anywhere so it is important to know how to help someone in need. Be aware of your messaging.

If you or someone you know is interested in taking a course to assist injured people following a traumatic event, contact your local public health department, hospital or clinic, emergency medical services, or fire and police departments to see if they offer any training. You can also look for local classes on the bleeding control, community emergency response teams, and medical reserve corps websites for additional information. Many teachers, administrators, and community residents feel the need to take such a class after surviving a mass shooting. One young woman I interviewed about the Parkland incident expressed how devastated, helpless, and guilt-ridden many felt because they did not know the correct protocol to assist the injured.

Another organization promoting citizen education in this area is BleedingControl.org, an initiative of the American College of Surgeons and the Hartford Consensus.[4] This organization advises, "Massive bleeding from any cause, but particularly from an active shooter or explosive event where a response is delayed, can result in death. Similar to how the general public learns and performs CPR, the public must learn proper bleeding-control techniques, including how to use their hands, dressings, and tourniquets. Victims can quickly die from uncontrolled bleeding within five to ten minutes." Their commitment to educating their community has become a critical necessity for our greater community.

ALICE: A Proactive Response

Many school districts have been using a program called ALICE (Alert, Lockdown, Inform, Counter, Evacuate)[5] to train their teachers, administrators, and students. ALICE goes beyond typical lockdown methods and is designed to provide individuals with a new set of skills that will greatly increase children's and school employees' odds of survival during a violent intruder event.[6]

Police officer Gary Crane created ALICE after the 1999 school shooting in Columbine, Colorado, because he felt that "locking down" or "sheltering in place" was not always the best option for students and employees in schools or businesses. Crane said that to him, the abnormally high number of people killed or wounded in mass shootings in the 1990s occurred in part because these lockdown responses made them easy targets.[7] He felt that teaching people to be passive observers might not always be the right response, as opposed to doing something proactive in order to survive. Teaching children to run and hide then wait for the police to arrive has proved deadly too often. He claimed that studies show in best-case situations, it takes police a minimum of five minutes to arrive at a school, but at times fifteen minutes or more.

---

[4] https://www.bleedingcontrol.org/about-bc

[5] https://www.alicetraining.com/our-program/alice-training/

[6] https://www.alicetraining.com/resources-posts/featured-videos/

[7] https://www.alicetraining.com/about-us/

The threat of an active shooter attack is rare but very real. ALICE hopes to eradicate the "it can't happen to me" mentality and change the way people in schools, universities, businesses, hospitals, and places of worship respond to armed intruders.

At the ALICE Training Institute, people are authorized and empowered to make their own life-saving decisions, and are trained in proactive response options, rather than a passive, mandated, one-size-fits-all response.

ALICE is part of a very large debate happening in our country: Despite its popularity, the majority of the schools I surveyed continue to use more traditional lockdown practices. Since the school shootings in Florida and in Texas, however, many teachers seem to be advising students to be more proactive in these situations.

My concern is that this can be confusing if different teachers in middle and high schools are giving their students choices of what to do or not do during a drill. It can become even more complicated when a child hears that there are many options for students when discussing drills with their siblings or friends.

Transparency and Protocol

School districts should have complete transparency regarding what protocols are in place, emergency training their teachers and administrators have received, and the kind of follow-up training planned. I recommend that you call your school district's superintendent's office to ask about this, then attend school board meetings with other engaged parents to advocate the programs and knowledge that will best protect your children.

Brad, the chief of police in a mid-size community, told me that he and several of his officers go to each school when there is a lockdown drill. He said that a tremendous feeling of angst and discomfort is slow to leave him on the days he attends the drills.

What about your child's school?

+ Make sure it has a plan and that everyone knows what they would do if confronted with an active shooter situation.

+ Teach your children to pay attention to school policy on identifying the two nearest exits when they are in the cafeteria or gym, to have an escape path in mind, and to find places they could hide.

+ Remind your child to follow the instructions given by the administration, but if something doesn't feel right to your child or she sees a way to escape, she should take it.

+ Make special arrangements if your child has a disability or other access and functional needs.

Evaluating Your School's Emergency Plan

Part of safety planning means knowing what to do should there be an event at your child's school. While different school districts have adapted their own protocols, following are some standard recommended measures. The National Association of Secondary School Principals has conducted crisis exercises and created guidebooks for schools.[8] Compare these with the plans that your school already has in place, and advocate change where you see fit.

1. **LISTEN** for directions from the teacher, the principal, and/or any adult in charge.

2. **RUN** and escape, if possible.

   - Getting away from the shooter(s) is top priority.

   - Leave your belongings behind and get away.

   - Help others escape, if possible, but evacuate regardless of whether others agree to follow or not.

   - Warn and prevent individuals from entering an area where the active shooter may be.

   - Call 911 when you are safe, and describe the shooter, the shooter's location, and weapons.

---

[8] "Conducting Crisis Exercises & Drills: Guidelines for Schools," National Association of School Psychologists, http://www.nasponline.org/resources-and-publications/resources/school-safety-and-crisis/conducting-crisis-exercises-and-drills.

3. HIDE, if escape is not possible.

- The teacher or adult in charge should lock and block doors, close blinds, and turn off lights.

- Get out of the shooter's view and stay very quiet.

- Silence all electronic devices and make sure they won't vibrate.

- Don't hide in groups—spread out along walls or hide separately to make it more difficult for the shooter.

- Try to communicate with police silently. Use text messages or social media to tag your location, or put a sign in a window.

- Stay in place until law enforcement gives you an all-clear signal.

4. Prepare your children (age appropriate) on what to do **AFTER** an event:

- Remain in hiding place until police give an all-clear signal.

- Keep hands empty and visible.

- Know that police officers' first task is to end the incident, and that they may have to pass injured people along the way.

- Understand that police officers will be armed with guns and may use pepper spray or tear gas to control the situation.

- Follow police instructions and evacuate in the direction they come from, unless otherwise instructed.

- If you are hurt, take care of yourself first, and then you might be able to help the wounded before first responders arrive.

- If the injured are in immediate danger, help get them to safety.

- While you wait for first responders to arrive, provide first aid. Apply direct pressure to wounded areas and use tourniquets if you have been trained to do so.

- Turn wounded people onto their sides if they are unconscious and keep them warm.

If You See Something, Say Something

This FEMA campaign engages the public in protecting our homeland through awareness-building, partnerships, and other outreach.[9] Always call 911 if you see something suspicious or unsafe. Teach your child the same thing. Better to be safe than sorry.

Instruct your children that when they report something to provide the following information:

+ Who or what they saw

+ When they saw it

+ Where it occurred

+ Why it appears suspicious

This is also a great opportunity to have another important conversation with your children about how important it is to be OBSERVANT. Talking points:

+ While walking down the street, don't walk with your head down staring at an electronic device or book. Keep your head up and stay aware of what is around you.

+ Talking on the phone while walking distracts you, making you less aware of your surroundings.

+ Trust your gut! If something does not feel right, there is a good chance it is not.

+ If you see something, tell someone: your parent, your teacher, a friend.

The Strength of Family

The goal of creating a family safety plan is not to frighten your children, but quite the opposite. Discussing practical contingencies and making everyone prepared for any possibility keeps you all safe. Listen to your family's concerns and then discuss them in a calm, thoughtful manner.

---

[9] "Do You Know the Signs of Suspicious Activity?" U.S. Department of Homeland Security, https://www. dhs.gov/see-something-say-something#.

I urge parents to have dinner or another meal as the setting for a weekly family meeting to check in, discuss important issues, and to go over the upcoming weeks' activities and technology time. It is during these meetings that you could periodically address your list of safety-related issues. You will be helping your child develop a sense of community and learn to listen and work collaboratively, all while building a strong sense of belonging and safety.

CHAPTER 8

Benefiting from Community

"The world is so empty if one thinks only of mountains, rivers, and cities; but to know someone who thinks and feels with us, and who, though distant, is close to us in spirit, this makes the earth for us an inhabited garden."
— Johann Wolfgang von Goethe

"The best way to find yourself is to lose yourself in the service of others." — Mahatma Gandhi

---

My research and experience as a therapist led me to conclude that stressed out, distracted parents and children can thrive by being part of a larger community. Community is something that provides safety, structure, and a sense of belonging. This kind of community appears to be dying in our current culture. Adults who came of age before the 2000s seem to have a different reference point when you ask them, "What was your community like when you were growing up?" I took this question to adults of all ages. Common responses included:

"We played outside until it was dark."

"My parents never knew exactly where we were or what we were doing."

"I still yearn for that sense of freedom, playing outside, wandering through the path in the woods with my friends."

"My best friend and I would save up our babysitting money for weeks. When we had a few dollars, we would walk more than a mile to town to buy something at the general store."

"I remember that if I skinned my knee or got locked out of my house, I went to a neighbor's house."

These days, the majority of children are growing up in an isolated, more physically protected but less physically active community than those who were kids even one or two generations ago. I believe that children thrive when they feel connected to a community larger than their family of origin; it is a significant factor in raising healthy kids.

Taking all of this into account, it is important that you ask yourself, "What type of childhood experiences do I want for my kids?" Family, community, neighborhood, religious affiliation, and volunteer activities are all part of what helps children feel like they are part of something larger than themselves. This sense of feeling connected, even if it is to just one or two trusted adults, helps kids feel less lonely. In addition, the feeling of contributing to something greater gives each child the chance to develop parts of their personality and identity. These community elements are critical in helping children build a strong, resilient foundation that will help them when they encounter difficult situations, including the lockdown culture in which they live, and anxiety over the "next" school shooting.

Family

For many people, the family is the first "community" they know, learn to navigate, and if they are fortunate, in which they feel safe and loved. The traditional "family" has changed. Today's family is more likely to be scattered than to live together in one place. Education and professional pursuits have created many more opportunities for people to live in different parts of the world.

I grew up in a small town in New Jersey surrounded by ten cousins, six aunts and uncles, and my grandmother, in addition to my parents and sister. Every week I spent time with some of my relatives. I still miss the Sunday night dinners that were a ritual for our extended family. Whether we were gathering at the local Chinese restaurant or the newest dining spot, we were all together. It was there, at the long table full of the cast of characters I loved, that I learned many life lessons. What I remember most about those days was the laughter, whether it was my dad sharing one of his famous stories of his adventures, or my cousins and I getting into mischief. I felt safe and loved. It provided me with a nurturing cocoon that helped protect me, guide me, and embrace me when I needed it most. It also taught me about tolerance, patience, and love. People had different opinions, and while they may have argued, they resolved issues and supported each other.

In the past thirty years of working with families, I have seen firsthand how quickly that particular community has shifted, leaving parents without the support and guidance of grandparents or other relatives. Parents have to be conscious of this shift and how they can recreate a sense of belonging for their children.

Spend Time Together

It is critical to spend time with your children on a regular basis. Carve out time to have at least one meal a day with them. If dinner is too complicated because of everyone's schedule, maybe start with a family breakfast. Make it a routine to all get together, without any technological devices, to enjoy a meal and talk. As my daughters were growing up, I chose to be the designated driver as often as I could. It wasn't ideal, but at least I had a few minutes to hear about their days. I tried to have a sense of humor about almost everything; finding moments to laugh and joke kept the stress down while building the bond between us.

Establish Family Meetings

Pick a time in the week to have a regular family meeting. We typically did it after those Sunday night dinners. I had a notebook handy to write down important dates and issues. I suggest going around the table so that each member can share what went well for them, or maybe not so well, in the previous week. I call it the "highs and the lows of the week." Start with the positive. Then each person can share something that was particularly challenging: what it was, why it felt so challenging, and how they solved it. (This is an incredibly important skill for children to learn—focusing on positive things, helping them to reframe negative situations into a challenging situation, and learning to realize they are capable of problem solving.)

If your child had a lockdown drill or related event, this is a time in which they can talk about it while having your undivided attention.

Go over the calendar for the following week, noting events for each family member. This helps children feel part of the family and creates a sense of calm when they know where their parents will be, who will be picking them up from practice, and what activities are on the calendar.

Helping children become functioning parts of the family is key to raising self-confident and self-sufficient adults who are well adjusted and can appropriately cope with frustrating situations.

Barbara H. Fiese, a clinical and developmental psychologist whose research focuses on family stated, "Mealtime conversations may include a cultural code embedded in the flow of conversations. These conversations highlight not only acceptable behaviors as in expectations for good manners, but also sociocultural norms."[1]

Give Children Chores

Responsibilities build strong character. During meals or family meetings, go over chores for the week. Remember to praise the act, not the child. For example, "I really like the way you kept your room clean this week," or, "I really appreciate that you babysat for your brother this week when I had to work late." By praising the *act*, you are acknowledging the child.

It works the opposite way, too. For example, "I am disappointed that the garbage did not get picked up this week. I thought we had agreed that taking out the garbage was your responsibility." With this approach, you do not insult the child but instead share expectations—a much healthier way to approach the issue. It also creates space for the child to respond.

---

[1] Fiese, Barbara H., *Family Routines and Rituals*, (Newhaven, Conn: Yale University Press, 2006).

Ultimately, you want to help your child learn to examine his or her own behaviors and choose to improve. If you decide that it is easier for you to just take care of the chore, you are reinforcing that you don't think your child is capable of doing things.

Don't be afraid to establish your family code. Together, talk about who you are as a family. Discuss your morals and the traditions you are building. This is all critical in helping a child develop a strong inner sense of who they are.

Neighborhood

The neighborhood is the next level of community. The concept of the neighborhood is markedly different today. In many communities, children rarely play outside. Life is much more structured. Children spend more time alone, plugged into electronic devices. This robs them of the chance to learn about different cultures, religions, and how other families function.

Depending on where you live, your work schedule, and culture experiences, your neighborhood may mean different things to your family. No matter where you live, it's important to focus on building a sense of belonging and safety in your child's life. If your child walks home alone after school to an empty house, create a safety net. Ask a trusted neighbor if you can give them a key in case your child forgets his.

Your neighborhood community, and your children in particular, will also benefit from these activities:

+ Get to know the parents of your kids' friends.

+ Host a barbecue for a few of the parents and kids.

+ Start a parent-child book club.

+ Invite parents and their kids to attend a sporting event or a concert with you.

+ Organize an international night, inviting guests to bring their favorite traditional food.

Kids feel safer when they know people that live in their community.

Volunteerism

Become part of the volunteer community. The benefits are enormous. Volunteering teaches even toddlers and preschoolers about compassion, empathy, tolerance, gratitude, and community responsibility. My experience is that children who volunteer are more likely to continue doing so as adults. Be the role model. Volunteer at your kids' school.

School Community

Getting involved in PTOs or PTAs is a good way to enhance your volunteerism. These opportunities are usually very local, and will have a direct impact on your children and their friends. You can get started by talking to your school's PTO or PTA leaders about joining a committee or project that you can do with your child.

At my daughter's preschool, parents were asked to select a "job" that would help out. My husband was in charge of the community garden plot. My daughter loved going with her dad on Sunday mornings to plant, remove weeds, and pick veggies.

Based on many of my conversations with parents, kids, and counselors, it appears that high school and college students are less likely to volunteer or give to charity today than they were fifteen years ago.[2]

While tragedies like school shootings or devastating hurricanes often spark immediate sympathy from young people, they don't necessarily lead to longer-term engagement, says Nathan Dietz, an associate research scholar who conducted a "Do Good" study along with Robert Grimm Jr.[3]

The "Do Good" study found that teenagers overwhelmingly volunteer through organizations with school-sponsored service activities leading the pack, and that schools may benefit from more intergenerational volunteering activities.

The study also found that adults between the ages of thirty-five and fifty-four showed an even sharper decline in volunteering than high

---

[2] Sarah D. Sparks, "Volunteerism Declined Among Young People," Education Week, July 17, 2018, https://www.edweek.org/ew/articles/2018/07/18/volunteerism-declined-among-young-people.html.

[3] Nathan Dietz and Robert T. Grimm Jr., "Doing Good by the Young and Old," https://nonprofitquarterly.org/2016/11/17/good-young-old-forty-years-american-volunteering/

school- and college-aged Americans, but teenagers whose parents volunteered were significantly more likely to do so themselves. Parents who volunteer raise children who volunteer!

Schedule volunteer time for you and your family. Put it on the calendar. Here is a list of volunteer activities you can do with your kids:

+ **Donate food to a food pantry.** Volunteer at a food pantry or homeless shelter once a month.

+ **Walk to raise money for a good cause.** Many organizations use walks to increase awareness and raise funds. Kids five and up can walk a few miles.

+ **Visit a nursing home in your area.** Ask if there are any residents who would like a visit. Many places can match you with one person to call on regularly.

+ **Respect your environment.** Pick up litter at a local park or while you take a walk in the neighborhood.

+ **Deliver meals.** You and your child can bring both hot food and companionship to homebound people through a local charity food service.

+ **Volunteer to be a driver.** Take your kids along when you drive elderly people or patients to their medical appointments or take nursing-home residents or isolated seniors to the grocery store or to visit friends.

+ **Play with pets.** Volunteer to care for abandoned dogs or cats at a local animal shelter.

+ **Volunteer for vacation!** I have spoken with families that go on volunteer vacations. There are a lot of resources online to learn more about this.

Advocacy Work

After the shooting in Newtown, Connecticut, many communities created "parents against guns" advocacy programs. After the shooting in Parkland, grassroots community organizations such as Moms Demand

Action for Gun Sense in America[4] and Everytown for Gun Safety[5] saw huge spikes in their memberships. I responded to a request for volunteers to start a Moms Demand Action group in my town. I could not remain quiet when parents were mourning their children. I needed to join others in the effort to protect them.

For me, sitting in a room with over 100 parents, counselors, and educators was inspiring and comforting. Mostly, it was healing. I was reminded that I was not the only one feeling terrible sadness.

Many parents not only supported, but encouraged their children's activism around gun laws. Students at Marjory Stoneman Douglas High School ignited an incredible movement that is hopefully waking up many complacent adults. Parents are inspired by the young people's passion. It is creating a climate of positive copycat behavior where kids are forming clubs in their schools, organizing walkouts, and learning to find their voices.

Parents also told me that witnessing all this activism reminded them of their own activist days. This is such a positive thing. Activism is an opportunity for parents and kids to be part of the greater community.

Spirituality in Your Home

Incorporating a sense of believing in something bigger than yourself can be the gateway to connecting to another community, whether it is based around a house of worship or a personal practice. How was your childhood home different than that of your children's? Why is it different? What are the benefits? Do you have any hesitations or resistance to bringing more spirituality onto your family life?

Have an honest conversation with your spouse/partner about your thoughts on religion and/or spirituality in your children's lives. Is there a place for organized religion in your home? This is a complicated question without a simple answer. Organized religion is on the decline. Millenni-

---

[4] https://momsdemandaction.org

[5] https://everytown.org

als are leaving organized religion at a faster pace than any other group in the last decade. More and more, children are growing up without identifying with a "formal" religion.

Many people believe that organized religion provides an essential element of spirituality. Belief in organized religion is intensely personal for each person and family. I believe that any form of organized religion can hold a very significant place in a child's life. It can give children context in which to learn right and wrong, a moral code, and a set of rituals. It can provide parents with assistance in creating a blueprint that includes family goals and objectives.

In my experience, organized religion provides boundaries that are often beneficial during teen years when it is common for young people to rebel and search for self-exploration. I have found that the child who has boundaries to rebel against doesn't have to go to extremes to experience a sense of freedom.

Organized religion combined with community service provides children a sense of belonging to something bigger than themselves, as well as to other people who share similar beliefs and traditions.

Poems or Prayer

If prayer or meditation is part of your children's lives, encourage then to use it during a lockdown. It may become part of their "tool kit" while they are waiting to find out if there is a real shooting occurring or if it is a drill. Or, help your child create a *mantra*—a word, a phrase, a sound or even a syllable—that can be repeated silently, over and over.[6] You can also suggest that he or she incorporate the breathing meditations I provided in Chapter 6, "Strategies to Help Your Child (and You) Cope" with this exercise.

Use what works for your family, whether it is prayer, meditation, or writing out your feelings in a letter or poem. This can help your kids be conscious, mindful, and present in their surroundings. This activity can

---

[6] Tris Thorp, "What Is a Mantra?" The Chopra Center, https://chopra.com/articles/what-is-a-mantra.

also help teach a child the concept of gratitude. Gratitude allows us to be present and aware of what is happening at the moment, and then to be aware that one is fortunate to have this moment, this friendship, this object, or this accomplishment. I feel that learning the art of being grateful is one of the most valuable gifts a parent can give their child.

Meditation, mindfulness, and prayer are tools that you and your family can use when violent natural or manmade events occur. You are equipping them to develop their inner dialogue. For more suggestions, see Chapter 6, "Strategies to Help Your Child (and You) Cope."

Mental Health Resources

I know you hear it everywhere, but it is true: Call 911 if you or someone you know is in or appears to be in critical physical or emotional distress!

For immediate support or intervention, call the National Suicide Prevention Lifeline (1-800-273-8255). Trained crisis counselors are available twenty-four hours a day. They are confidential calls. You can also go to or take someone to the nearest emergency room.

Numerous national agencies and professional organizations provide information on finding a mental health professional in your community. Examples include but are not limited to:

+ The **Anxiety and Depression Association of America:** is an international nonprofit membership organization dedicated to the prevention, treatment, and cure of anxiety, depression, OCD, and PTSD through education, practice, and research.[7]

+ The **Depression and Bipolar Support Alliance** envisions wellness for people living with depression and bipolar disorder.[8]

+ **Mental Health America** is a community-based nonprofit dedicated to addressing the needs of those living with mental illness and to promoting the overall mental health of all Americans.[9]

---

[7] https://adaa.org/who-we-are

[8] https://secure2.convio.net/dabsa/site/SPageServer/?pagename=dbsa_about_dbsa

[9] http://www.mentalhealthamerica.net/about-us

+ The **National Alliance on Mental Illness** is a grassroots mental health organization dedicated to building better lives for Americans affected by mental illness.[10]

Many university and medical school-affiliated programs often offer treatment options. Search on the website of local university health centers for their psychiatry or psychology departments. You also can go to the websites of your state or county government and search for the health services department.[11]

The National Institutes of Health states that some federal agencies offer resources for identifying practitioners and assistance in finding low cost health services. They include:

+ The **Health Resources and Services Administration (HRSA)** works to improve access to health care and provides information on finding affordable healthcare, including health centers that offer care on a sliding fee scale.

+ The **Centers for Medicare & Medicaid Services (CMS)** has information about benefits and eligibility for these programs and how to enroll.

+ The **National Library of Medicine's MedlinePlus** website has directories of organizations that can help in identifying a health practitioner.

+ The **Mental Health and Addiction Insurance Helpline** is a website from the U.S. Department of Health and Human Services that offers resources to answer questions about insurance coverage for mental health care.[12]

---

[10] https://www.nami.org/#

[11] https://www.nimh.nih.gov/health/find-help/index.shtml

[12] https://www.samhsa.gov/find-help/national-helpline

Additional resources include:

- The **Substance Abuse and Mental Health Services Administration (SAMHSA)** provides resources to help communities discuss mental health issues.[13]

- The **National Child Traumatic Stress Network (NCTSN)** was created to raise the standard of care and increase access to services for children and families who experience or witness traumatic events.[14]

- **National Center for Healthy Safe Children** is another organization that offers great resources and downloadable tool kits for parents and educators.[15]

Counseling

I have had the privilege of helping children and adults find comfort and healing through the guidance and support of a caring professional. I believe people aren't supposed to struggle or anguish alone. That is why there are people like me who are committed to helping those in search of finding a better, more comfortable existence.

If you feel that it may be warranted, don't hesitate to find a professional counselor, social worker, psychologist, or psychiatrist to work not only with your child, but with your entire family. Get recommendations for trained psychotherapists from your child's school, pediatrician's office, religious affiliation, or a trusted friend.

Embrace Your Community

I am grateful to the women in my life, especially my mother, who taught me how to step outside of my comfort zone and learn how to give to others. It is this sense of community that nurtured my soul and paved the path for me to become a social worker and psychotherapist. The act of joining with others for a greater good is a really wonderful thing. I

---

[13] https://www.samhsa.gov

[14] https://www.nctsn.org/about-us

[15] https://healthysafechildren.org/trauma-violence-and-school-shooting

encourage you to inspire your family in finding your path to building your community.

Community takes many forms. We all benefit when we explore new experiences, get involved, open our hearts, and create a strong and lasting sense of belonging. It always will be beneficial to you and your family and will build balance and resilience in the face of today's challenging realities.

CHAPTER 9

How to Talk to Your Kids After a School Shooting

"The first truth Buddha taught his disciples is that suffering is part of the human condition. If we simply try to avoid confronting painful experiences, there is no way to begin the healing process. In fact, this denial creates the very conditions that promote and prolong unnecessary suffering."

– Dr. Peter Levine, Ph.D. Healing Trauma[1]

Some days I feel like I am trained, just like Pavlov's dog, to respond viscerally whenever and wherever I hear or see the words "breaking news." I stop whatever I am doing and anxiously look up at the TV, listen to the radio, or read the alert that just posted on my phone. I brace to hear the latest tragedy, often one that includes gun violence, to befall my country.

In these moments, everything seems to be moving in slow motion except for my heart, which is beating so loudly I can hear it. My mind races in a split second, performing a mental scan—where are my daughters, my husband, and my extended family? Is everyone safe? "Breathe!" a little voice in my head shouts as I try to focus on what the newscaster is saying.

Years ago, I was speaking to a friend on the phone when she interrupted me, "A plane just flew into the World Trade Center. Turn on your TV." I'll bet you remember exactly where you were when you heard about that horrific attack.

---

[1] Peter A. Levine, Ph.D. *Healing Trauma, A Pioneering Program for Restoring the Wisdom of Your Body,* (Louisville, Colo: Sounds True, 2005).

Likewise, the "breaking news" announcement arrested my attention and I learned of a mass shooting at Sandy Hook Elementary School. I learned about the shooting in Parkland on Facebook.

According to CNN, on average there was one school shooting every week during the first six months of 2018. Noblesville, Indiana; Palmdale, California; Ocala, Florida; Raytown, Missouri; Lexington Park, Maryland; Birmingham, Alabama, and too many other places now must add their names to the ever-growing list of schools that have experienced some form of school violence.

All of these school shootings increase the level of concern and fear in children and school staff. In my interviews with teachers and students, I heard a variety of answers, but the common theme is that it's very nerve-wracking for all. Worrying if your school is going to be the next statistic is not healthy for anyone.

Is My Child Traumatized?

Traumatic experiences alter the way we think, we react, and the stories that we tell ourselves. Whenever I learn of the latest tragedy, my mind and body react the same way: The trained social worker and meditation teacher in me says, "Stop. Breathe while immediately accessing the situation." *I know how to react in a crisis*, I tell myself. I am one of those people who are usually good in crisis situations, especially when I am not in immediate danger. I think quickly, assess the situation, and immediately determine the "escape" route. I also can problem-solve many scenarios in a split second.

I used to explain that I was good in a crisis was because I am a trained social worker. But as the years have passed, working with survivors of all types of trauma, I have learned that my skill in dealing with trauma is because of those I survived as a child. My traumas may not have been obvious to my parents, teachers, or even most of my friends. Some were buried, and some were healed.

We all experience some traumas, known as *small ts*, and then there are major traumas known as *big Ts*. I tend to be hyper-alert, always have an exit plan, and worry a bit too much.

It is my experiences, both personally and professionally, that makes me feel the urgency to educate you about the risk of trauma.

Dr. Peter Levine is a respected therapeutic specialist who has been on the forefront of helping trauma victims heal and has trained thousands of therapists to assist their clients to do the same. He states that *trauma is about the loss of connection—to ourselves, to our bodies, to our families, to other people, and to the world around us. This loss of connection is often hard to recognize because it doesn't happen all at once. It can happen slowly, over time, and we adapt to these subtle changes without even noticing them.*

This is the lens I bring to you, the parent or the teacher, as I seek to help you work with children—not only after a traumatic event happens in our country or community, but in the current reality of children being traumatized with frequent lockdown drills.

In all of my research, there wasn't one student who didn't admit that he or she had some type of reaction from going through the lockdowns drills.

In the Aftermath

What happens to the thirteen-year-old who watched the live stream video of a high school student dying in real time? Or what happens to the high school student whose camp friend was killed in the latest school shooting? Kids see images of a teen bleeding out while some other student records this horror scene, a scene that I wish would only be saved for horror movies if they must be shown at all. What happens to the parents, siblings, friends, and grandparents who were worried sick about their loved ones, or who may now be grieving?

It's safe to say that all students are bothered profoundly by the events and drills surrounding the scourge of school gun violence. Even the students who initially stated that they weren't bothered by the drills would continue to add that a classmate or teacher was really upset during a drill.

What to Look For in Your Kids

"When our bodies are feeling uneasy, they give us messages," stated Dr. Levine. This is a basic concept that you can talk to your children about at an early age. Dr. Levine said the purpose of these messages is to inform us that something inside doesn't feel right and needs our attention. The first symptoms to show up after an overwhelming event (locally or far away, it doesn't matter) include:

+ **Hyperarousal:** This is indicated by an increased heart rate, sweating, a feeling that you can't catch your breath, tingling in your arms and legs, and muscular pain. It can feel like your mind keeps racing and/or having repetitive thoughts. For example, a voice rings out over the loudspeaker, "Lockdown, lockdown!" The child immediately worries that this is the real thing—that this time there is a shooter in the building. Thoughts trigger the body and the body starts reacting with elevated blood pressure, heavy breathing, sweating, and other symptoms.

+ **Constriction:** After a traumatic event it is common for a person to feel tightness in his or her body. The nervous system gets activated during the event or when learning about an event, making sure that as much blood as possible is available to the muscles in case you need to react quickly.

+ **Dissociation and Denial:** The term *dissociation* means that for a certain amount of time a person can lose connection with his or her thoughts, short-term memory, and even sense of identity. Dissociation protects a person from being overwhelmed by too much arousal, pain, and fear. It helps a person tolerate or even survive experiences that are too much to endure under normal circumstances. Denial is a different level of dissociation. When children deny that their parents just got divorced or a grandparent dies, they act as if nothing happened because if they did acknowledge it, the emotions might be too much for them.

The child may not be ready to talk about the event with parents, teachers, or friends.

In our fast-paced lives, parents and teachers need to be aware of symptoms that may alert them to a child who is suffering from trauma-related anxiety. Symptoms may show up or intensify after direct exposure to trauma or even distant trauma. These include:

+ Hyperactivity: A child (or adult) demonstrating an unusual amount of energy or an inability to sit still.
+ Hypervigilance: On guard, looking around, jumping at the slightest noise.
+ Extreme sensitivity to light and sound.
+ Sleep issues including nightmares and night terrors, trouble falling asleep, and difficulty sleeping alone.

Possible signs of trauma include:

+ Low self-esteem, feelings of shame
+ Feelings of guilt
+ Anxiety
+ Panic attacks
+ Seeking out dangerous situations
+ Fear of dying
+ Self-mutilation (self-inflicted cutting)
+ Stating they no longer believe in their religious or spiritual beliefs
+ Avoiding certain situations, activities, movements
+ A significant change in interpersonal relationships

If a person's trauma is not dealt with, possible symptoms that may show up a year or even several years later can include:

+ Immune system problems
+ Difficulty making commitments
+ Chronic pain
+ Depression

+ Chronic fatigue

+ Feelings of alienation and isolation

I was working with a high schooler who was experiencing a sudden onset of severe anxiety and depression. Partly because of my years of experience, or perhaps because of being entrenched in research for this book, I asked him his thoughts about school violence. He immediately told me he had often worried if he was in danger while in school, but after the shooting in Parkland, Florida, he really worried about it. "In fact, I think, 'could my school become the next school tragedy? After all, who really knows who will be next?'" He added, "I always know where the exit door is, and if a classroom has two doors I think about how I would escape."

As he talked, his forehead got sweaty and he was clearly agitated. I asked him, "Did your anxiety get worse after February 14?" (That was the date of the shooting in Parkland.)

He looked at me. "Yes!...I never realized the connection. Do you think that is why I am afraid to go to school?" The innocence in his voice struck me to my core. Yes, many children are being traumatized.

Tips for Dealing with a Traumatic Event

The first and best thing you can do when dealing with the aftermath of a traumatic event is to talk about what happened.

- Empower your kids by asking them direct questions. Ask them their opinions.
- Create a reasonable safety plan, which will not only help protect you, but can enhance your child's sense of feeling protected (See Chapter 7, "Helping Your Kids Feel Safe with a Family Plan").

For detailed guidance on this, see Chapter 5, "Talking to Your Kids About Violence."

Questions and Answers

Invite your children to sit down with you at the dining table or to take a walk together. Make it a priority to talk to your kids. If they don't talk, you do the talking. When discussing the event, always be honest! Give your child the opportunity to express their feelings. Don't overwhelm them with your own anxiety and do not dismiss their fears. Look them in the eyes and listen to their comments and questions.

Your introduction could be: "There was a school shooting in (_____) yesterday. It happened during classes. Did you hear about it? The shooter was a former student of the high school. Let's talk for a few minutes . . . I was so upset and scared when I learned about the shooting. What about you? Do you ever worry that there could be a shooting at your school?"

Pause. Wait. Look your child in the eye.

Or, "It is very upsetting to hear there was another shooting today. I heard about it on the TV. I was getting ready for work when I heard the breaking news report. Did you hear about it?"

Silence. Stay quiet for a few seconds.

Don't be afraid to share how you felt when you heard the news. Be candid and vulnerable. Children know when you are being honest and real with them.

Ask questions such as, "What did you think about when you learned about the shooting?" Or, "Did any of your teachers talk about it in school?"

Often, there will be additional police presence at schools for a while when there is a shooting anywhere in the country. This happens in case someone decides to be a copycat. This adds to the possible trauma.

"Do any of the kids think there could be a shooter in your school?" Manage your own emotions. It's okay for them to see you upset, but maintain your composure. Your kids are always watching you for clues of how to behave, especially in times of crises.

Don't be afraid or even wait for your child to bring up a conversation about a school shooting or gun violence. Ask, "Why do you ask?" or,

"What have you heard?"

You may hear this from your child: "Mom, do you think this could happen in my school?"

You answer could be, "I really don't think so. The principal and all the teachers are taught how to keep you safe. There is security at school. I get that it is scary. Let's focus on the positive: There are millions of school kids in the U.S. It is very unlikely that this would happen in your school."

Ask the question, "How do you feel when there is a lockdown drill?" Ask your child what he or she is seeing or hearing on social media, the internet, and television. You may want to limit TV viewing and be aware if it is on in common areas.

Overall, remember these baseline rules for talking to your child after an event:

- **Always remind your child that he or she is safe.** That yes, it is horrible that people lost their lives or were injured. Remind your child that there are roughly 50 million children in America who are fine. At times like this, it is critical that you help your child see that the chances of getting hurt are very small.

- **Give your child the opportunity to express their feelings.** Don't overwhelm your child with your anxiety and fears.

- **Don't judge their behavior.**

- **Be a good listener.**

- **Expect a variety of emotions and behaviors.**

For School Administrators: Steps to Reinforce School Safety

There are a number of steps school administrators can take to emphasize that schools are safe environments:

- Write an email to parents explaining the school's safety policies.

- State the crisis prevention plan in your community.

- Create a warm and welcoming presence at school, greet students and parents, and visit classrooms often.

+ Communicate the school district's efforts to maintain safe and caring schools.

+ Let the community know the behavioral expectations and consequences, if violated.

+ Provide crisis and preparedness plans.

+ Review communication systems within the school district and with community responders.

+ Provide crisis training that includes professional development for staff, not only of the physical responsibilities, but how to offer emotional support.

+ Stay up-to-date with current violence prevention programs and curriculum. Emphasize the efforts of the school to teach students alternatives to violence, including peaceful conflict resolution and positive interpersonal relationship skills.

+ Create a safety committee composed of administrators, teachers, and parents.

+ Educate parents and students about school counseling services that are available.

+ Educate parents and students about community mental health services that are available, including individual and group services.

School administrators must focus on the importance of creating a caring school community.

In addition to creating a caring school community, it also is critical that each student feels connected, understands expectations, and receives the behavioral and mental health support he or she needs.

Remember that communication with the community following a violent event reassures parents and students about the safety of their school.

What Teachers and School Administrators Can Say to Students

Designate specific times in class for teachers to talk with students about the recent incident. It must be communicated to teachers that it is necessary, and ultimately more important, than plowing through the scheduled lesson plan.

Listen to your students and validate their feelings. Let their questions guide what and how much information you provide, be open to opportunities to talk when they are ready, be honest about your own feelings related to violence, and emphasize the positive things that each child/family/school can do to stay safe. Be patient. Just like parents, keep yourself available for when they may want to talk. For example, if a student is hovering around the desk after class, or seems to be asking you questions you think they already know, assume it is difficult for them to let you know they are struggling and that they may not even understand why they are feeling bad. Some children can use writing, playing music, or doing an art project as an outlet. Young children may need concrete activities (such as drawing, looking at picture books, or imaginative play) to help them identify and express their feelings.

Be aware of signs that a student might be in distress, such as changes in behavior, anxiety levels, sleep issues, acting out, getting in trouble at school, or having problems with academic work. Also, be conscious of what kids are talking about, viewing on social media and the internet, especially regarding a recent event. Following are some suggested general key points when talking to students:

- Schools are safe places! School staff work with local police and fire departments, emergency responders, and hospitals to keep them safe.

- The windows are bulletproof glass (if true).

- Security guards are there to provide extra safety.

- Students need to play a role in the safety of the school. Urge every student to be observant and let an adult know if he or she sees or hears something that makes them feel uncomfortable, nervous, or frightened.

- Remind students that there is a difference between reporting, tattling, and gossiping. You can provide important information that may prevent harm either directly or anonymously by telling a trusted adult what you know or hear.

- Remind students to focus on the positive. Encourage them to participate in activities that they enjoy, stick to a routine, and be with friends and family to help make them feel better and to keep them from worrying about the event.

- Explain that, unfortunately, there are troubled people who are in such pain that they feel their only option is to inflict pain on others. They may be unable to handle their anger or may be under the influence of drugs or alcohol. Adults (parents, teachers, police officers, doctors, faith leaders) work very hard to get those people help and keep them from hurting others. It is important for all to know how to get help if feeling really upset or angry, and to avoid drugs and alcohol.

- Stay away from guns and other weapons. Tell an adult if you know someone has a gun. Access to guns is one of the leading risk factors for deadly violence.

- Be familiar with all counseling services available in the school. Refer a student to a counselor for additional evaluation.

- Reach out to the school counselor and parent if you have a concern about a particular student.

PTSD: How Do You Know If Your Kid Suffers?

Many people have heard about post-traumatic stress disorder (PTSD), a mental health condition that can be triggered by a terrifying event. It often is associated with soldiers who have been in war, but it can also affect anyone exposed to a school shooting or recurrent lockdown drills. Symptoms can include severe anxiety, uncontrollable thoughts about the event, flashbacks, and even nightmares. Additional symptoms include avoidance of everyday activities, being easily startled, lashing out at people, difficulty sleeping, loss of interest in previously enjoyable activities, and more. Sometimes these symptoms don't show up for weeks after an event. Dealing with PTSD is difficult, but with good care, people usually feel better in time. Getting effective treatment after PTSD symptoms develop can be critical to reduce symptoms and improve function.

You can find much more information on PTSD online including ways to tell whether your child may have it and how you may be able to deal with the situation. One website that provides good information is that of the National Institutes of Health, at https://www.nimh.nih.gov/health/topics/post-traumatic-stress-disorder-ptsd.

Other Sources of Support

Parent and student education is critical for support after a tragedy occurs locally or anywhere in the country. Here are some things that parents, teachers, and government officials can do to help ease anxiety, heal trauma, and nurture healthy kids.

- **A Community Forum:** The school district can offer a parent education workshop to talk about the mental health of children and parents.

- **Community Service:** You can encourage your young people to create a service project to help the community that was just affected by the shooting. Talk to them about the fact that school shootings are horrific, many children in this country have to deal with gun violence in their home environments and community, and what they can do to help. How can they get involved in helping advocate the safety of all children?

+ **Mental Health Parent and Student Programs**: Examples are the Mind-Body Skills Groups and the Center for Mind-Body Medicine.[2]

For example, parents in Parkland, who were qualified in facilitating mind-body training offered workshops for other parents, students, and teachers. There are many programs available to help both children and adults in the aftermath of a tragedy.

Healing After a School Tragedy

Schools utilize a variety of tools to help students deal with a violent incident, whether it happens at their school or another. These include:

+ Drop-in sessions with school counselors

+ School counseling forums

+ Educational seminars

+ Therapy dogs

+ Art therapy

+ Music therapy

+ Student-run vigils

+ Creating a memorial

+ Yoga programs

+ Meditation

+ Intergenerational programs—inviting seniors to come to school to tutor or read to young children

+ Mentor programs

These measures all can go a long way toward helping children heal, but keep in mind that it is very difficult to assess how children are doing and how well they will be in a week, a month, or even a year.

---

[2] https://cmbm.org

I have found that parents and educators are quick to dismiss my suggestion that certain life circumstances may be traumatic to a particular child.

Using my suggestions in this chapter, I hope that you will be able to add more items to your toolkit in order to address and handle traumatic events. The key to empowering your children is to have those difficult conversations!

CHAPTER 10

You Can't Heal Alone

Healing is a very personal, intimate experience. It means so many different things to each of us. What I do know, from both my personal and professional experience, is that you can't heal alone.

Mental health services play a key role in healing. Dr. Elana Regan, a psychiatrist at an outpatient drug and alcohol treatment center, has firsthand knowledge of this. She had dropped her husband off at the train station on September 11, 2001, having no idea it was the last time she would say goodbye to him and was just hours away from becoming a widow.

"It is incredibly important for survivors of any type of trauma to find healthy ways to process their stress and pain."

I asked Dr. Regan her thoughts on how a community heals. She told me that what kept her going, especially the first year, was participating in many community gatherings, vigils, memorials, and joining with other survivors in sharing their experiences. "Participating in ceremonies, even the simple act of lighting a candle, helped me get through the day," she said. Her voice got very quiet as she added, "I felt less alone because I knew there were others I could talk to about how I was feeling."

Dr. Regan notes that the body stores memory of traumas, causing physical symptoms as well as emotional symptoms weeks or even years later. Trauma-related symptoms may be delayed in occurrence, and the readiness to seek and receive support varies between individuals.

"You know, the body has a way of keeping score. It does not forget the trauma that the mind experienced," she told me. "It is incredibly important for survivors of any type of trauma to find healthy ways to process their stress and pain. This includes seeking professional assistance, when needed.

"Many children are not emotionally equipped with tools to help them cope," she continued. "Too often, they are the children who don't participate in chores, jobs, or activities in which they help others. These create opportunities for them to develop resistance and emotional integrity. Not having these experiences, and the resulting lack of healthy coping skills, can lead to addiction or other self-destructive behaviors."

This drives home the critical point that children should not be left alone with their thoughts and fears. As when preparing them for bad news and whatever may happen going forward, feeling connected to the family and the larger community is essential for healing.

Spiritual Healing

Robin, a mother of one of the Parkland shooting survivors, shared that after two and half hours of anxiously awaiting news that her daughter was alive, she finally received a text from her stating that a SWAT team had released her and a friend from their hiding place in a closet. "Mom, I am running to the synagogue. Meet me there," the text stated.

In this case, a house of worship became one of the first places to which a community reeling from gun violence looked to begin the healing process.

Rabbi Boxman: Becoming a Spiritual First Responder

On the day of the Parkland shooting, houses of worship became the front lines of healing. In the immediate aftermath, Bradd Boxman, Rabbi of Congregation Kol Tikvah, received a call on his cell phone telling him that his synagogue was in lockdown and that the gunman was still on the run. In fact, the synagogue also housed a preschool with close to 100 students.

"Rabbi, can you please get here as soon as you can?" asked his assistant. By the time he got to the synagogue, he already was in crisis mode. He said it felt like Ground Zero during September 11, 2001, when he had served as rabbi to a congregation with many congregants working in the financial district in New York.

He remembers that his actions after the Parkland shooting were similar to those he took on September 11. He launched into action, starting a phone tree, calling families to see who needed help. He also contacted members who were in the mental health profession to come assist immediately. He assumed correctly that the students and parents were going to need their community.

In all, twenty-six students from the synagogue community were students at Marjory Stoneman Douglas High School. Two of the preschool teachers had children who were students there. "Can you imagine two moms sitting together in the dark, trying to keep their students calm and quiet as they waited to hear if their children were alive?" he asked. Only one mother received a text from her child. Four from Congregation Kol Tikvah were killed on that dreadful day.

"We became the spiritual first responders. We became the rock that so many needed in those first hours, days and months," stated Rabbi Boxman. He described his community as "close-knit," where most people know each other. He also told me that even today you can still feel the loss wherever you go in town.

How does a community heal from such trauma? As I listened to him describe the many ways his community rallied together, provided much needed support and comfort to parents who had to bury their children, to siblings who mourned their brother or sister, to grandmothers and grandfathers who had to bury their grandchildren, to best friends who lost their best friends, I couldn't stop thinking, "How does a community recover from these darkest of days?"

Rabbi Boxman told me, "We continue to work with the other religious houses of worship to provide support for the community." In fact, at the time of our meeting, they were preparing for an interfaith service marking the six-month anniversary of the shooting.

It is heartbreaking that Rabbi Boxman and his community had to witness such anguish and cruelty, that they had to endure so much unbearable pain and trauma. I cry for parents who had to do the unimaginable, for the children who lost their lives, and for all who feared they were going to die.

Reverend Terry: Healing Through Collaboration

Terry Richardson, Pastor of First Baptist Church in South Orange, New Jersey, is one of the tallest men I know. Not only is he exceptional in stature, he also stands tall in his ability to impart wisdom and his devotion to helping every person he meets in his community. On December 14, 2012, a few days after the shooting at Sandy Hook Elementary School, in Newtown, Connecticut, I addressed his congregation on how to talk to your children in the aftermath of a school shooting.

"Parents need to acknowledge to their children who they are, what they think and dream about, and even what causes them to be distressed and anxious."

I was invited to speak at the church because of Reverend Terry's compassion and commitment to the emotional and spiritual health of his congregants. I helped him acknowledge they were struggling in the aftermath of such evil. He anticipated that the parents and children in his community where hurting, frightened, scared, and at a loss for how to discuss such evil with their children. When I addressed the congregation that Sunday morning, I saw mothers and fathers holding their children tightly. I felt the trepidation in the room as I attempted to help them acknowledge their fear, their pain, and find healthy coping strategies to assist their children in dealing with the news.

First Baptist Church continues to be devoted to providing not only its church members, but the larger community, with opportunities to join together in vigils, rallies, marches, and educational workshops. That is my definition of how a community continues to work on healing: not permitting people's religion, race, or sexual identity to limit them, but simply coming together for the human need for support and love. Fortunately, that is usually what I observe in the aftermath of a tragedy, but it's good to keep it in mind.

I asked Reverend Terry about his thoughts on how a community heals in the aftermath of continuing lockdown drills and school shootings. "It is all about collaboration, not staying in one's individual communities, but coming together as one large, powerful community," he explained. "Parents need to acknowledge their children for who they are, what they think and dream about, and even what causes them to be distressed and anxious."

He continued, "Parents need to remember what their job is—to raise children that are caring, kind, good people who are strong enough to survive what life gives them." He stated that often parents act like they have a short-term memory, forgetting their own struggles when they were coming of age. "Kids are dealing with so much, from environmental stressors to social and physical issues, that can all be challenging and scary. Parents need to provide direct support and guidance because this is what helps kids stay focused and better equipped to face so many issues.

"Parents need to strive to raise children who have a strong moral character, who take responsibility by helping their family and their community," he added. "When children have a sense of who they are and what is right and wrong, maybe students would not have to be hiding from danger in the corners of their classrooms."

Reverend Terry's message is clear: Parents need to devote time and energy to the development of their child's moral character. A community and all its members are stronger when parents are involved with their children. These actions enable the community to be more resilient after a tragedy strikes.

Preventative Care

Continually take the mental and emotional health temperature of your community. Is it the cultural norm for children and teens to complain about being stressed out and anxious the majority of the time? Is it the norm for parents to be unsure how to help their children navigate through endless hours of homework, after school activities, tutoring and lack of sleep? Do you, the parent, feel helpless that your child is suffering, and that he or she is experiencing panic attacks, wants to avoid school, is binge-watching YouTube and TV shows, and is over-indulging in drinking, drugs, or other at-risk behaviors?

What is your school community proactively doing to help their students, especially when they are traumatized from a shooting incident?

Many experts believe that mental health conditions can be prevented and mitigated. "Prevention builds on strong communities to protect individuals from declines in mental health. Prevention also reduces substance use, improves education outcomes, and boosts productivity," states the respected study. "The State of Mental Health in America 2018" was compiled by the Mental Health America organization, the nation's largest community-based nonprofit dedicated to addressing mental health issues. The organization provides services in schools, homes, and communities. The report also notes that that there needs to be psychoeducation and support provided to teachers and parents, as well as a promoting positive school climate.

During a recent parent forum, I addressed parents seeking assistance on how to help their children develop healthy coping strategies when dealing with too much stress in their lives. The parents in attendance had children who were in elementary school through college. The hard truth is that there are many factors contributing to the rise in anxiety and depression.

Fortunately, many schools throughout the country are consciously working with students to help them develop healthy coping mechanisms in their lives. Some schools have designated areas for kids to go when they need a mental break. They ask the teacher for a pass and go to a "quiet room" to sit on some bean bag chairs or a comfy couch and rest for a few minutes. Many schools have been incorporating mindfulness into their health classes, and even offering yoga as part of gym class electives. Schools are implementing longer lunch periods to give kids a chance to eat slower.

The establishment of mind-based programs is significant for communities building healthy foundations for children to feel safe and supported. This is especially helpful in times of crisis. There are school districts where starting times for middle school and high school are later in the morning, hoping that kids will benefit from more time to sleep.

There are many good ideas and programs available to communities. To start, find out what your school district is doing. Ask questions and get involved if you don't think they are doing enough.

Mental Health Screening Tests

Community healing critically depends on comprehensive and compassionate mental health screening and services, especially in public and private schools. The need for early identification and intervention for children at risk, and services and treatment for those in need, is greater than ever. According to research complied by Mental Health America (MHA), one in five adults has a mental health condition. Their key findings identify that mental health among youth is worsening, with severe depression increasing from 5.9 percent in 2012 to 8.2 percent in 2015. Still, 76 percent of youth are left with insufficient treatment or none at all, while 7.7 percent had no access to mental health services through their private insurance.

It is important to note that this research also found that there is a shortage of mental health care providers.[1]

Often, there are available resources, but schools and/or parents are not aware of them. For example, the MHA has numerous screening tests that you or your child can take online at MentalHealthAmerica.net. These can serve as useful tools to utilize with your child if you or they have specific concerns.

Breaking the Taboo: Becoming Stigma-Free

Individuals, schools, and governments all need to engage in healthy conversations about mental health. We need to eliminate mental illness as a taboo subject. Communities all over North America have started "stigma-free zone" initiatives dedicated to raising awareness of the disease of mental illness. These initiatives are designed to create a culture where residents who may suffer from any form of mental illness will feel supported by their community and neighbors. They typically bring together schools, local governments, mental health organizations, businesses, police departments, and of course, parents, in successful efforts to erase stigma. CarePlus New Jersey, a community mental health organization, has been a leader in this movement, helping to establish stigma-free zones all over Bergen County in the northeastern portion of the state. The website for the county's stigma-free initiative states that joining will:

+ Educate residents that mental illness is a disease and must be treated as such.

+ Raise awareness of the prevalence of mental illness in our community.

+ Provoke public interest in learning what is "stigma-free."

+ Provide residents with an opportunity to become involved in their community.

---

[1] http://www.mentalhealthamerica.net/issues/state-mental-health-america

+ Allow people living with the disease to feel supported by their community and thus decrease feelings of isolation and shame.

+ Link people in need to local mental health resources.

+ Raise awareness that care is accessible regardless of income.

Wherever you live, you can learn more about establishing a stigma-free zone in your community by calling CarePlus New Jersey at (201) 265-8200 or visiting the Bergen County Stigma-Free Zone webpage, where you can download a tool kit.[2]

Healing Through Acknowledgment and Understanding

At all times, but especially in the difficult aftermath of a violent event, parents and school officials need to clearly and honestly discuss the fear surrounding school shootings among themselves and with their children. My own suggestions for this include the following:

+ **For Education:** I encourage all schools to have an education forum on school safety at the beginning of each school year. Parents should be made aware of the safety procedures, alert system, teacher training, and any other useful information.

+ **For Students:** A few times a year, school administration should provide updates on school lockdown drill protocol. School counselors should be specifically trained to lead discussions with students on how to discuss the emotional consequences of the drills. They must be trained to identify students who may need additional counseling to cope with their anxiety and fear.

  - Create a safe place, such as the school counselor's office, for students to go when feeling sad, stressed, and need a safe place to talk or just relax.

  - Hold group sessions led by a trained counselor. Parent and student educational workshops help teach healthy coping

---

[2] https://www.co.bergen.nj.us/mental-health-services/stigma-free-zone

skills—groups help people to not feel so alone in their fears and anguish.

- Encourage peer support.

- Provide advocacy opportunities for students to get involved in.

- **For the Community:** Communities need adequate funding for mental health programs in schools and the greater community. It is necessary to have crisis counselors, psychiatrists, and other professionals available, not only immediately after a shooting occurred in a specific community, but as a permanent part of available services.

The bottom line is this: Your community will heal by acknowledging that there is a problem—that there is pain. Acknowledge that some children are hurting, and then substantiate their experiences, creating a sense of safety and hope. Be proactive and creative, think outside the box, and talk to your kids about their thoughts and feelings in order to construct a healthy, caring community.

However, don't simply assume that you really know how children are feeling and thinking. If you find yourself making that assumption, stop and reflect on how your younger self would have felt going through a similar experience. Sit with that feeling, and then work to create ways to support children growing up in the shadow of gun violence.

Make time to go over their social media accounts with them. Review who they are friends with, what is being posted by them, and those they follow. This is a good way to stay abreast of what they are thinking and feeling.

Talk to the parents of your kids' friends. Check in on how they are doing. Make a deal that you will keep them in the loop on how your kids are doing. Share this with your kids. Discuss which adults in the community they can trust and can talk with as needed.

Remind your community's children that the trauma and angst they may be experiencing is normal—that a tragic event is upsetting to everyone. Normalize their feelings. Tell them that it is not unusual to be fearful, angry, frustrated, have trouble trusting adults, jump at any loud noises, not want to go to school some days, or cry at the strangest of times. Remind them it is normal to worry that a shooting could happen at their school—or even if they are preoccupied with death and dying and feel like studying makes no sense right now. This is common.

Healing is a complex, lengthy process, but with attention to these strategies, you will make things better for all of our children. You will be able to provide them with emotional health and resilience as they deal with the news reports and fears that are everywhere in our culture—and especially the event that they must deal with again and again in school: waiting to find out if the lockdown is just a drill or the real thing.

Where Do I Sign Up for a Healthy, Compassionate, Resilient Kid?

There is no doubt that parents, educators and even elected officials need to focus on the mental and emotional well-being of our children. Students, parents, and staff are being traumatized in this climate of fear and lockdown drills. The question is not only to what degree is it traumatizing, but how can you, the parent, help minimize the negative effects of raising your children in the climate of fear?

A huge dilemma facing public and private schools is the fact that there really is not a foolproof way for them to succeed in this current atmosphere of school shootings and drills. Alarmed parents, concerned school boards, and school administrators are all confronted with the same question: What is the best way to keep our children safe?

- Bulletproof windows, armed security guards, and police officers are questionable solutions.
- Teachers carrying guns does not solve the problem.
- Endless lockdown drills and evacuation drills are not keeping our kids safe.
- Changing the protocol from children huddling in a corner of a classroom to students running and hiding, searching for a safe space, still is not working.

There is no guarantee that hiding in a dark classroom, locking doors, or even planning ways to attack the shooter will work.

The problem is that there is no simple answer. Tragically, there is no guaranteed 100-percent safe environment for students and teachers today.

We are a country that is focused on preventing school violence by focusing on external threats. Given that, who is focusing on the internal struggle that all of this madness is causing for our children, from the youngest of our students to those in college?

Our country is experiencing a spike in teen depression, anxiety, and a proliferation of harmful behaviors. The epidemic use of alcohol, marijuana, and vaping is yet another symptom that our youth are not coping with all of the stressors that exist. During adolescence, teens are flooded with hormones that only serve to only enlarge and magnify their experiences and thoughts.

I encourage you to carefully consider all of the factors of school violence and its potential impact. There are three basic areas to consider when you are striving to raise a resilient, kind child: your child's physical, emotional, and mental health.

Nurturing Physical Health

Your child's physical health includes proper diet, exercise, and sleep. A well-balanced diet is extremely important for a child's developing brain and body. I am a huge proponent of a diet that is based on real, unprocessed foods. Processed foods are anything that is not in its original form. For example, non-processed foods are nuts, milk, apples, applesauce, rice, and veggies. These are all "real" foods.

Processed foods typically come in a box or package such as kids' cereal, rice cakes, candy, chips, and so on. I always recommend organic when possible.

Of course, everything in moderation. Helping a child learn to enjoy a variety of food early on makes it easier when they become teens. Limit sugary food and drinks. From a young age, teach your child to choose to drink their sweet or eat it. Prohibit combinations such as soda/juice and a cupcake. Another tip I used with my daughters: If you can't pronounce the ingredients, they probably don't need to be in your body.

Exercise is very important. Simply moving your body is an excellent way to release built-up tension and emotions. Regular activity is key. I have seen an increasing number of children and teens resistant to exercise, even walking. It is critical for children to have time to play freely and to enjoy moving their bodies. In addition, endorphins are released during the process and exercise helps to balance out hormones during puberty.

It is critical for children to have a good night's sleep. This means they get the requisite hours of uninterrupted sleep recommended for their age. Most parents are quick to admit that their children are sleep-deprived, yet many are unwilling to muster up the courage to do something about it. Do it. Sleep helps heal the mind and the body.

Observing Emotional Health

Whether related to the fear of school violence or anything else, it is always a good idea to pay attention to your children's habits and behaviors. Notice if their appetites have changed, if they are having a hard time falling or staying asleep, experience an increased number of nightmares, show resistance to doing things they used to enjoy, express new fears and anxieties, or display a new preoccupation with death, guns, or self-harming behaviors.

Trust your parenting instincts. If something doesn't feel right, talk to your children! Don't hesitate to take them to a professional just to be safe.

Ask yourself this: Are your children growing up in a family that provides them with an opportunity to experience their feelings? Do you allow your children space and time to learn about their own emotions? Is there the kind of flexibility in your family that allows them to have their experience without you projecting your own anxiety on to them, or needing to control their behavior?

For example, perhaps your son loses an important baseball game. He obviously is very upset, so you instinctively jump in and start telling him how to feel. "Don't worry, you will win the next one" or, "It's not your fault you lost, it was that other kid. Did you see how bad he pitched? No wonder your team lost the game."

Stop. Let your child have the space to be quiet, cry, or yell. Still, set boundaries as needed. If a child is carrying on for too long, say, "It's okay that you are angry. Why don't you go take a walk or run outside and blow off some steam?"

Ensuring Developmental Health

How can you help your child develop age-appropriate problem-solving skills? One girl participating in a lockdown drill called her dad from the closet of her high school, telling him she was going to die. He told her, "You are going to be okay. We have been preparing for the time when you needed to take care of yourself. You have the skills. Stay focused on surviving." This is a great example of a parent helping his child not only prepare, but rely on herself.

A child who is in kindergarten or first grade is not developmentally able to process what it means to be prepared for a school shooter. You need to use age-appropriate words to help them practice safety measures while still protecting them. Think of the example of the little girl in Marin County, California, who was told that they practice lockdown drills in case a wild horse becomes lost and gets into their school. This is an age-appropriate way of helping kids practice listening skills in case of a real emergency without flooding them with fear.

The mental component can become very complex when it comes to dealing with middle school and high school kids who are in the midst of hormonal earthquakes. Hormones can wreak havoc on an otherwise healthy, well-adjusted kid. Kids' resiliency is challenged by hormone surges which makes them all the more vulnerable to crisis, and requires you to have a methodical, sensitive approach in communicating with them.

Navigating Today's Environment

Parents can help a child navigate these troubling times by preparing them for the adolescent years. For example, a mother of a pre-adolescent daughter talks to her about what to expect when she gets her period, how her body will change, and how she may have emotional and physical symptoms. If any men in the household don't act like the changes of puberty are fodder for teasing or shaming and instead remain supportive and kind, it will help a girl to grow up with a sense of confidence and acceptance.

Words and actions matter. The right approach helps build the foundation of resiliency that enables a teen to handle the bumps that life throws their way.

How well a young person is able to handle or bounce back after a crisis depends on his or her foundation. The child with fewer prior traumas will more than likely deal with post-traumatic stress in less time. It could affect one child for six or eight weeks, while for another healing could take years. "Eventually, [a school shooting] is going to happen here," was a statement I heard from many students over and over again when I conducted interviews for this book.

During a conversation with a school board member discussing her district's safety procedures to prevent school violence, specifically school shootings, I was informed that her district had installed bulletproof windows several years ago. A few weeks later, during an interview with a police detective from the same community, I asked how the community decided to install the windows. He seemed confused. "We don't have bulletproof windows," he told me. "We installed protective shields on the windows in the schools. The shields stop the windows from shattering, but do not stop a bullet."

I wish I could say that this type of miscommunication was rare, but I found many inconsistencies regarding safety protocol. In some communities, between administrators and staff, police and school administration, or parents and children, there often was confusion and frustration with the information disseminated.

The fact that there continues to be consistent miscommunication in many communities is a direct result of schools, police, and parents all being in a *reactive phase* of figuring out how to keep students alive.

We need to accept that this is the new reality, as ugly and terrifying as it may be. This is where we are right now. Facing the challenge head-on is critical in order to begin to have honest and productive conversations about the short and long-term damage it is causing to children.

This national discussion about school safety must be expanded to focus on not only how to keep our children physically safe, but emotionally healthy.

I have heard unbearable pain in the voices of innumerable survivors of school shootings. The message from many of the survivors' families is that you just don't know the effects of trauma.

Matthew, a high school student, made sure to tell me recently that he had a lockdown drill. "It was really scary—you could tell it wasn't the regularly scheduled drill. We all ran to our hiding places and just waited. Finally, we were released. It turned out there was a fire in the school basement. It is sort of funny how a having a fire in your school now comes as a relief."

Countless variations of this scene continue to play out over and over again throughout our country. Remember, your best strategy to help your child is to talk to them about their experiences. Evaluate how you think they are coping with all this stress, and seek help when needed. It is critical to help children develop healthy coping mechanisms to deal with the current state of affairs.

Giving Kids "Space" to Regroup Emotionally

I followed up with Jack a few months after our first interview to see how he was doing as a fifth grader. He and I sat with his aunt (a family physician), and his grandmother (a pediatrician). As we discussed my work on this book, Jack's grandmother and aunt were surprised to learn that kids were not only enduring lockdown drills but were struggling with them. That's when Aunt Jane asked, "Jack, what do you think about hiding during a lockdown drill?"

Jack sat up in attention and answered in a loud voice, "I am used to them by now." He launched into a long story about how there was a crazy girl outside his school last year threatening to do something bad. "We had to go into hiding. The police came. Remember Mom, when that happened?" Mom nodded.

I asked Jack how he felt after the drills were over. Jack looked at me as he stated, "I can't go back to my seat after the drill. I go to get a drink of water from the fountain; I walk the long way around the room, and finally sit down. I just can't sit right back down." He added, "Mom, don't be mad at me—it's just too hard to sit down right away."

I was quick to wipe my tears away as I answered, "I get it . . . I get it."

I excitedly explained that I thought he was brilliant for coming up with a strategy to give his mind and body a chance to regroup before he had to start working again.

I hope that this book helps to educate both parents and teachers on the need for children to have SPACE before they return back to work after a lockdown drill.

We Need to Do Better

We, the adults in our country, need to do better than this. We *must* do better.

My advice, as I note throughout the book, is to stay informed. Know your child's school safety policy, and specifically, the lockdown drill protocols. Give your child some undivided attention; listen and talk about his or her experience of participating in lockdown drills. Find creative and direct ways to have open and honest conversations with your children.

Please don't be timid in your efforts to find out what your kids are doing on their electronic devices. Maybe you allow your child to have an Instagram account at age twelve as long as you are one of his or her followers. Setting firm and consistent boundaries may be hard at the moment, but in the long run they will help your child develop a stronger sense of right, wrong, and endurance.

Now is a really good time to participate in community activities. Encourage your children to find something they are passionate about, do some research, and get involved.

I am most grateful to the brave souls who spoke with me, who allowed me to open up old wounds, who trusted that by sharing their stories I could help you understand the necessity of dealing with this issue. It was their stories, shared with me in total anonymity, many forever imprinted on my mind, that drove me to help you understand the magnitude of what is happening to too many kids, and how all of us can help them grow up safe and well-adjusted.

Month after month, I admire these kids' bravery in the face of regular active shooter and evacuation drills, waiting to know if each one is the real thing or not. I acknowledge and honor their feelings, their reactions, and their fears. There is a lot we can learn from these stories.

Teach your children not to hold on to their fears. Teach them that talking about fear, finding ways to express it, and then learning to let it go is the path to healing. Reminding children that they don't have to be scared is how we teach them to be resilient and strong. It gives them the feeling of being in control.

It is my hope that schools will partner with parents to face the challenge of keeping children safe in today's uncertain world.

As a therapist, it is my passion, and yes, my job, to serve as a vessel of sorts, a place where people feel safe to share their most intimate, painful struggles. Together, we embark on an expedition to uncover, problem-solve, and create a set of skills to help them heal and grow. It continues to be my privilege to be that anchor and launching pad for so many. I set out with a goal to hear what is really happening to our greatest resource, our children, in this new reality, one to which we all must awaken and must discuss in the most thoughtful and responsible way possible.

I asked the hard questions. Then I listened to the words of children.

To the brave young man who raised his hand during a school program I was facilitating and requested, "Can you please ask my mom to put down her phone and listen to me when I am talking?" I respond that I will continue to try to help parents understand what is at stake.

This is my best plea to you: Not only pay attention to what is happening in your child's life, but be present. Monitor your own anxiety; take care of yourself so you can take care of your children.

I promise you the rewards will be worth it.

About the Author

Nancy Kislin is a Licensed Clinical Social Worker, Certified Marriage and Family Therapist, keynote speaker, author, and former Adjunct Professor at Kean University. She maintains a private child, adolescent, and family psychotherapy practice in Chatham, New Jersey. She creates and facilitates parent, teen, and children programs in schools, religious institutions, and summer camps. As a speaker, Nancy has addressed diverse audiences ranging from small groups of parents and school students classes, to religious institutions, educators, and other psychotherapists. She has always been at the frontier of bringing current issues confronting children and parents to her audiences.

Nancy is passionate about helping parents and children navigate the complex issues of today's society. She hopes to ultimately inspire them to lead productive, joyful, well-balanced lives. She lives in Central New Jersey with her husband.

nancykislintherapy.com
 Nancy Kislin, Parenting Educator
 NancyKislin

Index

Credits

Publisher: Michael Roney

Art Director: Sarah M. Clarehart

Cover Artist: Richard Turtletaub

Copyeditor: Heather Pendley

Proofreader: Katharine Dvorak

Indexer: Karl Ackley

Made in the USA
Middletown, DE
05 May 2021